teach® yourself

javascript

mac bride

for over 60 years, more than 40 million people have learnt over 750 subjects the **teach yourself** way, with impressive results.

be where you want to be with **teach yourself**

For UK orders: please contact Bookpoint Ltd., 130 Milton Park, Abingdon, Oxon OX14 4SB. Telephone: +44 (0)/1235 827720. Fax: +44 (0)/1235 400454. Lines are open 09.00–18.00, Monday to Saturday, with a 24-hour message answering service. You can also order through our website www.madaboutbooks.co.uk.

For USA order enquiries: please contact McGraw-Hill Customer Services, PO Box 545, Blacklick, OH 43004-0545, USA. Telephone: 1-800-722-4726. Fax: 1-614-755-5645.

For Canada order enquiries: please contact McGraw-Hill Ryerson Ltd, 300 Water St, Whitby, Ontario L1N 9B6, Canada. Telephone: 905 430 5000. Fax: 905 430 5020.

Long renowned as the authoritative source for self-guided learning – with more than 30 million copies sold worldwide – the *Teach Yourself* series includes over 300 titles in the fields of languages, crafts, hobbies, business, computing and education.

British Library Cataloguing in Publication Data
A catalogue record for this title is available from The British Library.

Library of Congress Catalog Card Number: On file.

First published in UK 2003 by Hodder Headline Plc, 338 Euston Road, London, NW1 3BH.

First published in US 2003 by Contemporary Books, A Division of The McGraw-Hill Companies, 1 Prudential Plaza, 130 East Randolph Street, Chicago, Illinois 60601 USA.

Typeset by MacDesign, Southampton
Printed in Great Britain for Hodder & Stoughton Educational, a division of Hodder Headline Plc, 338 Euston Road, London NW1 3BH by Cox & Wyman Ltd, Reading, Berkshire.

Impression number   10 9 8 7 6 5 4 3 2 1
Year   2007 2006 2005 2004 2003

contents

preface

JavaScript is one of the key programming languages of the Web – and the easiest to get to grips with. What makes it so easy? There are several things. First, the language is quite small – it contains a limited number of objects and methods. While this does restrict what your programs can do, it also means that you can soon learn it all. Second, JavaScript is embedded in HTML, so that you can start by adding small routines to tags to create special effects, and gradually increase the size and complexity of your code. Third, JavaScript requires no special software – all browsers can handle it, so you need nothing extra to develop or run programs.

This book is aimed at people who understand HTML, but have little or no programming experience. *Teach Yourself JavaScript* is not intended to give a full, in-depth coverage of the language, but to introduce the main concepts and techniques. It concentrates on the practical uses of the language and largely ignores the theoretical basis and the details of the syntax.

If you do not know how to use HTML, could I ask you to spend a weekend working through my *Teach Yourself HTML* (or a similar introductory book by another author, if you must!) before starting on this book.

Enjoy your programming!

Mac Bride
macbride@tcp.co.uk
Summer 2003

01
introducing javascript

In this chapter you will learn

- about JavaScript and HTML
- about types of programming languages
- how to start learning JavaScript

What is JavaScript?

JavaScript is a browser-based programming language. Its code is written directly into the HTML of Web pages and is interpreted and executed in response to some activity on the page – such as when loading is complete or a button is clicked.

JavaScript interacts with the browser. It can read information off the Web page, for example, data entered into the fields of a form. It is aware of the objects on the page and knows when things happen to them – it doesn't just pick up the obvious things like mouse-clicks, but it also notices when a browser window is active and when the focus moves to a different window. And it is these events that trigger the execution of code – in programming jargon, JavaScript is an *object-based, event-driven* language. It can write onto the current browser window or a newly-opened one – and it can write standard HTML code, so that you can use JavaScript to generate Web pages in response to activites in a Web page.

JavaScript is not a particularly complicated language and there are limits to what you can do with it. At the simplest, a piece of JavaScript code may do no more than display a message box to acknowledge that a button has been clicked. At the other end of the scale you can use JavaScript to write complex interactive games (though not fast shoot-'em-ups) or to check an on-line order, calculate the costs and produce a confirmation form. Its limitations arise mainly from the fact that all its inputs and outputs must go through the browser and it cannot store data in files.

Client-side and server-side JavaScript

This book only covers client-side JavaScript – that version of the language which is written in Web pages and which runs within the browser when the page is viewed. There is also a server-side version of the language – one which runs on the computer where the Web page is hosted. That requires the co-operation of your ISP. For client-side JavaScript you need nothing but a browser, a word processor and some effort and imagination.

What does JavaScript look like?

JavaScript can be incorporated in a Web page in four ways:

* Written into the body of a page in <SCRIPT> tags;

* As attached code, written into an HTML tag;

* As a set of functions (named blocks of code) written in the <HEAD> area;

* As a set of functions written into a separate text file, and brought into the page through a link.

You can have any combination of the four in a page. You can also use JavaScript variables as values in tags.

<SCRIPT>

Code can be written enclosed in <SCRIPT> tags. This is the simplest way to get code onto a page, but it has two major limitations. The code is executed just once, when the page is loaded, and it can only refer to those objects that are already on the screen – if it tries to access something on a part of the page that has not yet been downloaded, the code will crash.

```
<SCRIPT>
    alert("Hello from JavaScript")
</SCRIPT>
```

This script produces a message in an alert box – the standard box used in Windows applications to prompt the user.

Attached code

JavaScript commands can be written directly into those HTML tags, such as those that produce buttons or other objects on a form, that can have suitable events – it's the event that sets the JavaScript going.

Here's a simple example. This creates a button, and when it is clicked, a message is displayed in an alert box.

```
<HTML>
<HEAD>
<TITLE>Code in a tag</TITLE>
</HEAD>
```

```
<BODY>
<FORM>
<INPUT TYPE = button VALUE = "Click Me" onClick =
"alert('Ouch!')">
</FORM>
</BODY>
</HMTL>
```

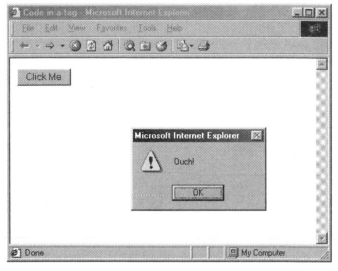

Figure 1.1 The display when the button is clicked.

Focus on the last phrase in the <INPUT…> tag:

```
onClick = "alert('Ouch!')"
```

This follows the standard shape for in-line JavaScript:

```
event = "JavaScript statement(s)"
```

The event in this case is **onClick**. This activates the statement:

```
alert('Ouch!')
```

Notice that the script is written in double quotes, and that the text within it – 'Ouch!' – is written in single quotes.

There can be any number of statements in the same script. They should be separated by semicolons and the whole set must be enclosed in double quotes. This will display two alert boxes, one after the other:

```
<INPUT TYPE = button VALUE = "Click Me" onClick =
"alert('Ouch!'); alert('Please stop!!')">
```

If you want to test this, type the HTML code into your word processor or text editor, save it as a text file, calling it *test.htm* or something similar, then open it in your browser.

Functions

Though these in-line blocks can be as big as you like, anything more than two or three statements is hard to read and prone to error. In-line code is best kept short and simple. There is a better way to handle more complex code.

A function is a named block of code, which you can call into action from another piece of code.

```
<HTML>
<HEAD>
<SCRIPT>
function showmessage()
{
    alert("Ouch!")
    alert("Please stop!!")
}
</SCRIPT>
</HEAD>
<BODY>
<FORM>
<INPUT TYPE = button VALUE = "Click Me" onClick =
"showmessage()">
</FORM>
</BODY>
</HTML>
```

This code does exactly the same as the previous example. When the button is clicked, the function *showmessage()* is called. This is defined in <HEAD> area and will produce two alert boxes, one after the other.

When there are only two statements, the advantages of a function are not very obvious, but above this, the little extra typing that is needed to set up the function is a small price to pay for the clarity of well laid-out code.

Notice the shape of the function. All functions have the same general pattern:

```
function function_name() {
    statements
    statements
}
```

The keyword function is followed by the function name, which has () brackets after it. These brackets may contain data which is being passed between the function and other parts of the code. The statements are held together by {curly brackets}. The convention is to write the opening bracket directly after the function name(), and the closing one on a line by itself at the end. The statements are normally indented by one or more tabs.

In practice, it doesn't make any difference how you lay out your code – except for readability. These layouts would work just as well. I prefer the first layout. If the opening and closing brackets are both by themselves at the starts of lines, it is very simple to glance down the code and make sure that each opening bracket has its matching closing bracket.

```
function function_name()
{
    statements
    statements
}
```

```
function function_name()
{   statements
    statements }
```

Files of code

Here's the same code again, but this time handled as a separate file. The file consists of the same code that is written in the function, but without the <SCRIPT> tags. It is saved in plain text format, with the extension .js.

Here's *ouch.js*.

```
function showmessage()
{
    alert('Ouch!')
```

```
            alert('Please stop')
    }
```

The code file is brought into a Web page using the SRC option in the <SCRIPT> tag. The functions in the file can then be used by calling them, as normal. Here's the revised Web page:

The code file is brought into a Web page using the SRC option in the <SCRIPT> tag. The functions in the file can then be used by calling them, as normal. Here's the revised Web page:

```
<HTML>
<HEAD>
<SCRIPT SRC = ouch.js>
</SCRIPT>
</HEAD>
<BODY>
<FORM>
<INPUT TYPE = button VALUE = "Click Me" onClick =
"showmessage()">
</FORM>
</BODY>
</HTML>
```

In practice, you would not use a separate file for something as trivial as this. A file makes sense where you have functions that you want to use in several pages. By writing them into a file, you only have to type them in and test them once, but you can use them as often as needed.

Programming languages

The only language that a computer can understand is *machine code*. This consists of numbers that the chip translates directly into commands, values and memory addresses. The commands are extremely simple; e.g. 'move this value into this memory address', 'compare these values', 'add 1 to this value'. Every type of computer has its own version of machine code.

In the early days, when computers were much simpler, people wrote programs in machine code. No one does nowadays – it's very hard work and there are better ways to write software.

Programming languages use words and structures that are (more or less) comprehensible to humans. The programmer writes instructions as a text file – known as the *source code* – which is then converted into machine code for the computer. There are basically two ways of doing this.

Compiled languages

Some programming languages are *compiled*. The source code is passed to a *compiler* program, which first checks the text for errors, and stops if it finds any. The programmer must sort them out before the compiler will go to the next stage and turn the text into the machine code of an executable program.

The program will only run on the same type of computer on which it was compiled, because different types have different hardware and use different machine code. If you want to run the same program on different types, such as Windows and Linux PCs and Macintoshes, you can – in theory – take the source code across and recompile it. In practice, the code will normally need some rewriting because each machine tends to do some things in its own special ways.

Interpreted languages

Source code can also be *interpreted*. An *interpreter* takes each line in turn, checks it for errors, then – if it's error-free – converts it to machine code and executes it. As with the compiled languages, you normally have to rewrite the source code to transfer a program to a different platform.

JavaScript is an interpreted language. Unusually – and happily for us – the same code will work on any type of computer, as long as it is running a reasonably modern version of Internet Explorer or Netscape Navigator (anything from 4.0 onwards). The interpreter is built into the browsers, and it's the browsers that handle the differences between hardware platforms.

Starting JavaScript

Any piece of JavaScript code normally has all or most of these elements:

- one or more objects on the page, and an event relating to an object
- some stored data
- statements which create its structure
- calculations or other processing of data.

Objects

JavaScript sees a web page as a collection of objects. Images and the buttons, text boxes and other components of forms are all objects, as is the page itself and the browser window that it is in.

* All objects have *properties*, such as colour, position or the text that they hold.

* Most objects have *methods* – ready-made routines which are used for manipulating the object.

* Most objects have *event handlers* – routines which are triggered when the object is clicked or changed in some way. These can be used for activating JavaScript code.

The next chapter introduces browser objects, their properties, methods and event handlers. Once you have got to grips with those you can start to write code that will interact with the browser and visitors to the page.

JavaScript objects

There are other JavaScript 'objects' – Array, Date, Math and String – which are really just collections of methods. We will leave these until Chapters 3 and 5.

Stored data

If you want to carry data from one part of a program to another, or keep it safe while other things are happening, it can be stored in *variables* – named memory locations. They are not needed if your code does no more than simple interaction with the browser page, but to go beyond this you need to be able to handle stored data.

Chapter 3 will introduce variables.

Program structure

A program consists of one or more statements – lines of code. At the simplest, the statements will be executed once, one after the other. But there can be lots more to it than this, which is where the fun comes in programming. You can get the code to loop back, so that a set of statements are repeated many times – to process a mass of information or to create some kind of cumulative effect. You can write code which checks values and runs in different directions, depending upon the result.

We shall be looking at ways to control the flow of a program in Chapter 4.

Calculations and methods

You can do a wide range of data processing with JavaScript. As well as simple arithmetic, it can handle a wide range of mathematical functions, manipulate text in many and varied ways, calculate time and dates, and sort or otherwise process blocks of data.

Arithmetic calculations are covered in Chapter 5. The methods used in processing maths, text and dates are introduced in Chapter 5.

Putting it together

In the second half of the book, we will draw all these elements together to explore some of the ways in which we can use JavaScript to create active and interactive pages.

Learn by doing

The best way to get to grips with any programming language is to play with it. Try all the sample code given in this book. First type it in exactly as given, then explore the concepts and techniques by varying the text, values, sizes or other aspects. When you are clear about how each new element works, combine it with what you learned previously and write your own pages.

You do not need any special software for JavaScript – just a browser and a text editor. I use Internet Explorer and Notepad. I use Notepad for three reasons – it has all the editing facilities I need; it's a small program and so is fast to load; and it's what is used by the **View > Source** command in Internet Explorer to display the page – which is very handy.

Test procedures

You will find your own way of working after a while, but here's how I test code – you may like to do the same.

1   Write the first program page in your text editor and save it as *test.htm* (or something similar).

2   At the start of later working sessions, open your test page in your browser.

3   Use **View > Source** to open the page in your text editor.

4   Edit and rewrite the code to test the next idea.

5   Save the edited file – use **File > Save** or click the **Save** button.

6   Go back into Internet Explorer.

7   Click the **Refresh** button to reload the page.

8   When you do produce something that you want to keep for future use, simply save it with a new name, then go back to *test.htm* for the next test.

Using the same file and flicking between the text editor and the browser in this way is quicker and simpler than opening and closing different files.

Comments

Try to make your JavaScript code readable. When you come back to a page after a few days, weeks or months, you shouldn't have to struggle to make sense of it. Giving meaningful names to your variables, functions and objects will help, and may be enough with short pieces of code. If your code is longer or more complex, you should add comments to remind yourself what is stored in variables and how routines work.

There are two ways to write comments.

•   For a short note at the end of a line or on a line by itself start with a double slash:

```
// num holds 5 at this point

num1 ++; // num now holds 6
```

- To write a comment several lines long, start the first line with /* and end the last line with */

```
/* e-mail address checking routine
First check that the text box contains text!
Then check for @ in the address
Last check for spaces and invalid characters */
```

Summary

- JavaScript is a browser-based programming language. Its code is written in the HTML of Web pages.

- JavaScript code can be written into a tag or directly into the body of a page, or written as functions in the <HEAD> area or in a separate text file.

- Code normally runs in response to a button click or other event.

- A function is a named block of code, which you can call into action from another piece of code.

- The text of programming languages has to be turned into machine code for the computer.

- Any piece of JavaScript code normally has one or more objects, an event to trigger it off, some stored data, statements to create its structure and some form of calculations or other processing.

- Adding comments to your code will make it more readable.

Netscape and other browsers

Internet Explorer is not the only browser, though it is far and away the most popular – which is why I have used it to test the examples in this book. If you use Netscape or any other browser, you may find minor differences in the way that JavaScript is interpreted.

02

objects and events

In this chapter you will learn

- about JavaScript objects
- how objects are named
- about properties and methods
- how event handlers can trigger JavaScript code

JavaScript objects

An object is a bundle of routines and values that define its appearance (if it is visible) and its interaction with other objects and the rest of the program.

Most JavaScript objects are visible parts of the HTML system – buttons and text areas, forms, frames, windows, even the page itself. Some objects are abstract, and are there to provide extra facilities to JavaScript. These include String (for holding text), Date (for finding and setting the time and date) and array (for managing groups of objects). There is also a Math object, which is essentially a collection of trigonometry and other mathematical functions and constants.

Whatever the type, all JavaScript objects have **properties**, most also have **methods** and **event handlers**.

*   **Properties** define the object. Typical properties are width, height, colour, and status. All can be read and some of them changed by JavaScript code. For example, this would turn the page (document) background red:

    document.bgColor = red

*   **Methods** are built-in routines which work on that object to which they belong. For example, the document object has a *write* which you use to write on the page:

    document.write("Hello from me")

*   **Event handlers** are routines that pick up actions that affect the object. Buttons, for instance, have an **onClick** event handler that knows when the reader has clicked it. Much of the JavaScript code that you write will start from one of these event handlers.

Object names

If you need to read or set the properties or value of an element, or move to another frame or window, you must be able to identify it. There are two aspects to identifying an object in JavaScript – where the object fits into the scheme of things, and its given name, if any.

Objects exist in a hierarchy, with smaller ones contained within larger ones. A **window** has (optionally) **frames**, then a **document**. This may contain **forms** which hold **elements** such as **text inputs** and **buttons**. The document may also contain **images**, **targets** and other elements.

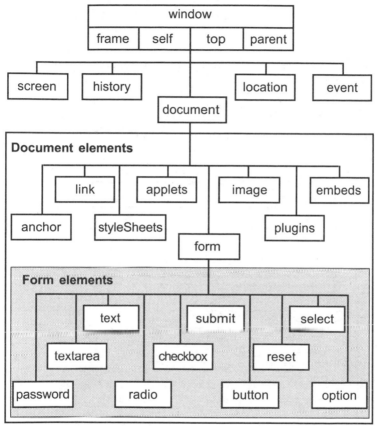

Figure 2.1 The browser object hierarchy.

The larger objects – windows, frames and documents – are automatically named as 'window', 'frame' and 'document'. You only need to use names if you have more than one of that type in the pages that are used by the program.

Other objects need names if they are actively used by the script – you will come across examples of this later, particularly where we are working with form elements and images.

Rules for names

Names must be single words, must start with a letter and may contain any combination of letters, digits and the under_score.

* JavaScript is case-sensitive – upper and lower case characters are not the same. 'Button1', 'BUTTON1' and 'button1' are three different names.

You will make life easier for yourself if you keep names simple. Stick to lower-case letters, using capitals only where you have compound names, where capitals mark the start of each word, e.g. 'surname', 'price', 'address1', 'totalCost', 'mailToMe'.

With short scripts, you can get away with numbered names – 'button1', 'button2', etc. With longer ones, you should make your names more meaningful – 'startButton', 'stopButton' and the like.

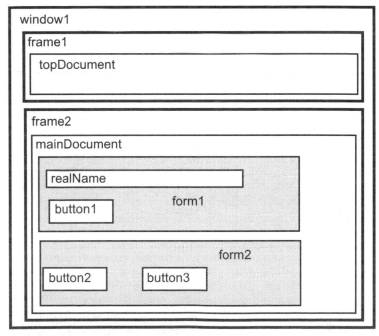

Figure 2.2 Naming objects.

Names and the hierarchy

An object's name is created from its place in the hierarchy – the structure of the web page. Look at the page in Figure 2.2. It has two frames, and the document in the bottom frame has two forms.

If your code was in a document in *window1*:

* to refer to the document in the top frame you would use *frame1.topDocument*.

* to refer to the *realName* text box, you need the rather longer *frame2.mainDocument.form1.realName*.

Note the full stops used to separate the parts of the name.

If the code was in a document in another window, you would need to add *window1* to the start of the name, hence:

* *window1.frame1.topDocument*

* *window1.frame2.mainDocument.form1.realName.*

Names can get a bit long-winded, but that's JavaScript!

Assigning names

We've seen how JavaScript refers to objects on Web pages, but how do they get their names in the first place? The answer lies in the HTML coding. The tags that create these objects all have a NAME option, and it is there that names are assigned.

Try this example. The HTML here creates a form containing a button and a text box. The form is produced and assigned the name 'myForm' by this line:

```
<FORM NAME = form1>
```

The text box is created by this line:

```
<INPUT TYPE = text NAME = output>
```

As this is inside *form1*, which is inside the document, it will be referred to by JavaScript as *document.form1.output*. This is the relevant line, in the <SCRIPT>. It writes inside the text box by setting its *value* property (see below). The property is tacked to the end of the name:

```
document.form1.output.value = "This is JavaScript"
```

The button does not need a name, as the script will not be referring to it, but it does need an onClick to start the code:

```
<INPUT TYPE = button VALUE = "Click Me" onClick =
"respond()">
```

Here's the complete code for the page. Type it in and try it.

```
<HTML>
<HEAD>
<TITLE>Names </TITLE>
<SCRIPT>
function respond()
{
    document.form1.output.value = "This is JavaScript"
}
</SCRIPT>
</HEAD>
<BODY>
<FORM NAME = form1>
<INPUT TYPE = button VALUE = "Click Me" onClick =
"respond()">
<BR>
<INPUT TYPE = text NAME = output>
</FORM>
</BODY>
</HTML>
```

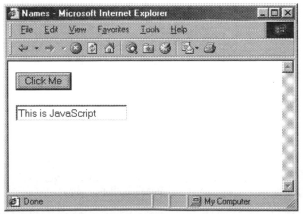

Figure 2.3 The page after the button has been clicked.

Let's see how JavaScript can read from objects, as well as write to them. We will add another text box, using it to collect the name of the visitor to the page. We'll call it *visitor*.

> Please enter your name: <INPUT TYPE = text NAME = visitor><P>

The active part of the script is now:

> document.form1.output.value=document.form1.visitor.value

This takes whatever has been typed into the *visitor* text box – its *value* – and writes it into the *output* text box.

```
<HTML>
<HEAD>
<TITLE>Names </TITLE>
<SCRIPT>
function respond()
{
document.form1.output.value=document.form1.visitor.value
}
</SCRIPT>
</HEAD>
<BODY>
<FORM NAME = myForm>
Please enter your name: <INPUT TYPE = text NAME =
visitor>
```

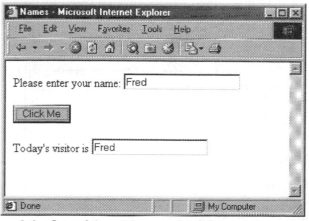

Figure 2.4 One of the main ways in which JavaScript can interact with visitors is by reading and writing data on forms.

```
<P>
<INPUT TYPE = button VALUE = "Click Me" onClick =
"respond()">
<P>
Today's visitor is <INPUT TYPE = text NAME = output>
</FORM>
</BODY>
</HTML>
```

Properties

Most of the time you want to refer to a **property** of an object, rather than the object itself. In the last two examples, for instance, we have been reading and changing the *value* property of the text boxes.

Text properties

The properties which an object has vary with the nature of the object, but generally reflect the attributes that can be set with options in the HTML tag. The *Text* object, for example, has these properties:

defaultValue   same as VALUE = and is what will be written in the box when it first appears

form property the name of the form that contains the object

name   same as NAME =

type   same as TYPE =

value   same as VALUE =, or whatever has been entered into the text box on the page

In practice, *value* is the only property of a text box that is used much in scripts.

Document properties

The document object has far more properties than a text box, though you are not likely to use many of these unless you get into some really heavy scripting. One thing to note here is that there are three different types of properties. The first set reflect the options of the <BODY> tag.

alinkColor	same as ALINK =
bgColor	same as BGCOLOR =
fgColor	same as TEXT =
linkColor	same as LINK =
vlinkColor	same as VLINK =

The second set has information about the page in relation to the Web site.

cookie	defines a cookie
domain	the domain name of the Web server where the document is stored
lastModified	the date a document was last modified
URL	the full address of a document
referrer	the URL of the linking document, if any
title	same as the <TITLE> tag

The third set of 'properties' are actually arrays of objects (see page 41 for more on arrays), and offer an alternative way to access these objects. There are arrays of anchors, applets, plugins (the *embeds* array), forms, images and links. We will be looking at some of these further on in this book.

Changing document properties

The next example produces a page with a little bit of text and two buttons. Clicking the buttons will change the colours of the page. Type it in and try it. Once it is working properly, add another button and related function code to restore the normal colours.

```
<HTML>
<HEAD>
<TITLE>Document properties</TITLE>
<SCRIPT>
function blackwhite()
{
    document.bgColor = "black"
    document.fgColor = "White"
}
```

```
function colour()
{
    document.bgColor = "red"
    document.fgColor = "yellow"
}
</SCRIPT>
</HEAD>
<BODY BGCOLOR= white TEXT = black>
<H1>Document Properties</H1>
<H2>Click a button to change the colour scheme</H2>
<FORM NAME = myForm>
<INPUT TYPE = button VALUE = "B/W" onClick =
"blackwhite()">
<P>
<INPUT TYPE = button VALUE = "Colour" onClick =
"colour()">
</FORM>
</BODY>
</HTML>
```

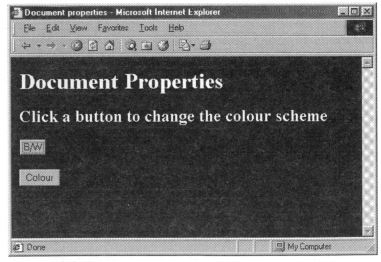

Figure 2.5 The screen display after clicking the B/W button.

Colour names

To set colours, use the standard names – see page 154.

Properties of other objects

We will look at the properties of the other form elements when we cover forms in Chapter 6. Of the other major objects, we will deal with images in Chapter 7, and windows and frames in Chapter 8.

Properties and the hierarchy

The links between objects in the hierarchy are properties: *button2* is a property of *form2*, which is itself a property of *mainDocument*. This also works up the hierarchy: *form2* is a property (parent of) *button2*. This can be useful as you will see once we start getting into some real code.

Methods

A method is a ready-made function that belongs to an object. Most of the methods are found in the special 'objects', Date, Math and String (see Chapter 5), but the browser objects also have some. All form elements, for example, have these two methods:

focus() moves the cursor into a text box or highlights a button, checkbox or other option

blur() is the opposite of **focus()**

This example shows the **focus()** method in action on buttons. When you click one of the buttons, another one gets the focus. It's all done with in-line scripts in lines like this:

```
<INPUT TYPE="button" NAME = button1 VALUE="Button
1" onClick="button2.focus()">
```

Two things to notice here:

- The method has empty brackets after the name. In other methods, the brackets are used for passing data to the method or getting information from it. Here there is no data to transfer but the brackets are still essential as they indicate to JavaScript that **focus()** is a method.

- The button's full name is the *document.form1.button2* but we can get away with the short form as the script is attached to *button1* which is in the same form as *button2*. If the same code had been written as a function in <SCRIPT> tags, the full name would have been needed.

Type in the code and try it. To convince yourself that the code really does move the focus, change the numbers so that the focus is moved to different buttons.

```
<HTML>
<HEAD>
<TITLE>The focus() method</TITLE>
</HEAD>

<BODY>
<FORM NAME = form1>
<INPUT TYPE="button" NAME = button1 VALUE="Button
1" onClick="button2.focus()">
<INPUT TYPE="button" NAME = button2 VALUE="Button
2" onClick="button3.focus()">
<INPUT TYPE="button" NAME = button3 VALUE="Button
3" onClick="dbutton1.focus()">
</FORM>
</BODY>
</HTML>
```

We will look at some of the other form element methods in Chapter 6.

write() and writeln()

These two document methods are used for displaying text (and other material) on the page. They are both used in exactly the same way and have virtually the same effect. **writeln**() puts a newline character – an [Enter] keypress – after the text, but HTML usually ignores it.

The basic shape of the **write**() method is:

document.write(*expression, expression,...*)

You must specify a *document*. If you are writing to the current page, then use a simple 'document'. If the output is going to a different page, you must also include the name of the frame or window.

```
MainFrame.document.write(...)
MessageWindows.document.write(...)
```

An expression can be a string of text, a number, variable or the value returned by a function. A single write() can have any number of expressions – separate them with commas.

The text that you write can include HTML tags, and these are interpreted as normal by the browser before displaying. Which means that you can use the method to produce formatted text, <HR> lines, links, images or any other Web page material.

Note these next points carefully!

◆ If the write() is written into a script in the <BODY>, it is performed as the page is loaded, and its output appears on that page.

◆ If the write() is in attached code or a function and is activated by a click or other event, the page display will be complete before it runs. When it is performed, the output will replace the current page, unless it is directed into another frame or window.

You can see both of these in the next example. Look for the <SCRIPT> at the start of the body, and see how its document.write puts text on the screen. (Though in practice you would never use it in this way as it is much simpler to use the normal tag.)

The *output()* function will pick up the name written in the text box (*form1.visitor.value*) and say 'Hello' to it. Notice the tags in the second write() that push the text onto a new line and embolden 'interactive'.

When it is working, experiment with other text and tags.

```
<HTML>
<HEAD>
<TITLE>The write() method</TITLE>
<SCRIPT>
function output()
{
    document.write("Hello ", form1.visitor.value)
    document.write("<BR>Welcome to my <B>interactive
      </B> page")
```

```
}
</SCRIPT>
</HEAD>

<BODY>
<SCRIPT>document.write("<H2>Using write() to write
HTML</H2>")</SCRIPT>
<FORM NAME = form1>
<INPUT TYPE = text NAME = visitor>
<P>
<INPUT TYPE = "button" VALUE = "Click Me" onClick =
"output()">
</FORM>
</BODY>
</HTML>
```

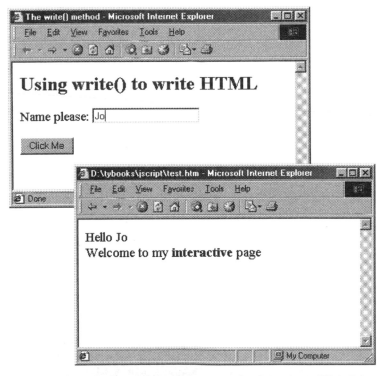

Figure 2.6 write() creates a new page for its output. Click the browser's Back button to return to your test page.

Event handlers

Web pages are active and interactive. Files and images load in, the visitor moves between frames and windows, enters text, makes selections and clicks buttons. These events can all be picked up by *event handlers* and used to start JavaScript code.

There are 13 event handlers:

onAbort applies only to *images*, and indicates that the image file has stopped loading.

onBlur applies to all screen objects – *window*, *frame*, *button*, *checkbox*, *password*, *radio*, *reset*, *select*, *submit*, *text*, *textarea* and *fileUpload* – and is activated when the object goes out of focus.

onChange applies to *text*, *textarea*, *select* and *fileUpload* picking up each keystroke or change of status.

onClick applies to the form elements *button*, *checkbox*, *radio*, *reset* and *submit*, and to *link* and *area* (linked area on an image map).

onError applies to *window* and *image* and is activated by an error during downloading.

onFocus applies to all screen objects – *window*, *frame*, *button*, *checkbox*, *password*, *radio*, *reset*, *select*, *submit*, *text*, *textarea* and *fileUpload* – and is activated when it comes into focus. For a window this means when it is opened; for a form element it initially means the topmost one, then the one that the user moves into with a mouse click or by pressing [Tab].

onLoad applies to *window* and *image*. For a window, onLoad is activated when download is complete. For an image, onLoad occurs when the SRC property is set in an <IMG> tag – this is not the same as downloading. Images can be downloaded and stored in memory, then allocated to <IMG> tags later. With animated GIFs, onLoad occurs every time the animation starts. See Chapter 7 for more on images.

onMouseOut	applies to *link* and *area* (on an image map).
onMouseOver	applies to *link* and *area*.
onReset	applies only to *form*, and is activated by a click on the *reset* button.
onSelect	applies to *text* and *textarea*, and is activated when the user selects part or all of the text
onSubmit	applies only to *form*, and is activated by a click on the submit button.
onUnload	applies only to *window*, and occurs when the window is closed or the user moves to another window.

Writing in the Status bar

The next example shows two of these event handlers at work. It also introduces a new object and a new method. Let's look at those first:

```
self.status = 'Hello and welcome'
```

This line sets the Status bar to read 'Hello and welcome'.

self is a window object, and refers to the current window. This could have been written as **window.status** and would have worked in exactly the same way. Where there are several windows, **self** simply makes it clearer which one is being used.

status() is a method which sets the contents of the Status bar. For reasons which I have not yet fathomed, if you use this with onMouseOver, you must add the statement 'return true' at the end to make it work. When a function or method ends, it can pass data to the code which called it through its return value (see page 79). We are not using the return value here, and you do not need this if you start status() in any other way. So, you need it here:

```
onMouseOver = "self.status = 'Click and visit'; return true"
```

but not here:

```
onMouseOut = "self.status = 'Go back and click me!!!'"
```

Notice that onMouseOver and onMouseOut are in the same tag. You can have any number of event handlers in a tag.

```
<HTML>
<HEAD>
<TITLE>The Status bar</TITLE>
</HEAD>

<BODY>
<SCRIPT>self.status = 'Hello and welcome'</SCRIPT>
<FORM NAME = form1>
<INPUT TYPE="button" VALUE="Click Me"
onClick="self.status = 'Thank you for clicking'">
</FORM>
<A HREF = www.theplace.com onMouseOver =
"window.status = 'Click and visit'; return true" onMouseOut
= "window.status = 'Go back and click me!!!'">This is a
link</A>
</BODY>
</HTML>
```

Type in the code, save it and view the page in your browser. What happens to the Status bar when the page first opens, when the button is clicked, when you pause over the link and when you move off the link? Now, change the first line of JavaScript code to read:

```
self.defaultStatus = 'Hello and welcome'
```

The *status* method sets the Status bar until it is changed by something else. *defaultStatus* has a more permanent effect. It defines what is there unless it is being actively changed. Edit the line and test the page again. You will find that the Status bar message reverts to 'Hello and welcome' after you click the button and when you move off the link.

Escaping characters

This is not about jailbreaks! Characters such as " and ' have a special purpose in JavaScript. But what if you want to show them on the screen? The answer is to write a backslash (also known as *escape*) in front of them. JavaScript then treats them as normal printing characters. e.g. this line:

```
document.write("He said, \"You\'ve got to visit \'http\\\\:
www.tybooks.com\'.\" ")
```

Produces this output:

> He said, "You've got to visit 'http\\: www.tybooks.com'."

Notice that you can also display a backslash if you write another one in front of it.

See page 156 for a more on special characters.

Exercises

1 Create a form with three buttons and one text box. Set up a separate function to be activated by the buttons, each writing a different message into the text box.

2 Extend the document properties example (page 21) to give it two more colour schemes – lime green text on dark blue, and white on white. When might it be useful to have the background and foreground in the same colour?

3 Use the write() method to create a page with <H1> and <H2> headings and at least two separate lines of text.

Summary

- JavaScript objects have properties, methods and event handlers.

- The name of an object depends partly on its place in the window/document/form hierarchy.

- Different objects have different sets of properties

- To identify a property of an object, give its full name with the property name appended.

- You can read and change the properties of objects from within JavaScript.

- A method is a ready-made function. All methods belong to, and normally act upon, objects.

- Event handlers respond to the events that occur to objects. They can be used to trigger JavaScript code.

03 variables

In this chapter you will learn

- how to create, name and use variables
- about calculations in JavaScript
- about storing and handling data in arrays

Variables

Variables are named places in memory where you can store the data for use in programs. You can have as many variables as you need, and call them what you like – within the rules for names (see next page). When you run the script, the system will allocate space for the variables, and convert the names into the memory addresses that the computer uses.

Here *Sum* holds 145, *x* holds -99 and *visitor* holds 'Jo Bloggs'. These values can be changed at any point either by the script or by the user entering data.

Variable name	Memory
Sum	145
x	-99
visitor	Jo Bloggs

Unlike most programming languages, JavaScript does not mind what type of data you store in a variable – the same can be used, at different points in the code, to store numbers, text or other values.

There are essentially three types of data:

numbers JavaScript does not distinguish between integers (whole numbers) and those with decimal fractions – you can mix and match them as much as you like. Numbers are normally handled in the denary (base 10) format, though JavaScript can read values in octal, hexadecimal and other bases.

strings Any text written in quotes in the code, or typed in by a user is a string. It can consist of any number of characters from 1 upwards – if there is a maximum, I have never run up against it.

Boolean These are either *true* or *false*. They are mainly used for carrying the results of a test from one part of the code to another.

A variable can also hold *null*. This is used to refer to empty strings and missing objects.

Creating variables

Variables should be set up, or *declared*, using the keyword **var**.

```
var visitor
var max = 500
```

The first line creates the variable *visitor*, but without giving it a value; the second creates *max*, and assigns 500 to it.

You can also set up a variable at any point in a script by simply assigning a value to it:

```
x = -99
message = "Thank you for calling"
```

These lines set up a variable called *x* with a value of -99, and one called *message* holding the string "Thank you for calling".

Where variables are used to hold important data, or to transfer data from one part of a program to another, it is good practice to declare them at the start of the program or of the block of code in which they are used. When you come back to your code after a few weeks, it will be easier to understand if you can see at a glance what variables are used in the program and what their initial values are.

Variable names

The rules for variable names are the same as those for object names. Names must start with a letter or underscore (_) and may contain any combination of letters and digits. Spaces cannot be used and symbols should be avoided. You may not use any of the reserved words (see page 155). Keeping names short and simple will reduce typing errors, but the most important rule is that names must mean something to you!

You can use either upper or lower case letters in a name, but mix them with care as JavaScript is case-sensitive. *myName*, *myname*, *MyName* and *MYNAME* are four different things. The convention is to use capitals only at the start of following words in a multi-word name.

```
ageLimit = 18
sex = "M"
var VATdue
```

Assigning values

To assign a value to a variable, use code of this pattern:

```
variable = value
```

The value can be:

* a literal – some text, or a number, or the words *true*, *false* (with Boolean variables) or *null*;

* another variable;

* a calculation or other expression;

* a function or method that produces a value.

Displaying variables

Variables can be used wherever you can use text or numbers. You can write them on screen, or display them in text boxes on forms or in dialog boxes (see page 56).

```
document.write(sum)
```

This will write the value of *sum* on the page. If you want to display the variable with some accompanying text, they can be joined together by the + sign.

```
document.write("The total is " + sum)
```

Notice that there is a space *inside* the quote at the end of the text. This is needed to separate the text and the variable when they are written to the screen. Miss it out and you will get:

```
The total is999
```

The scope of variables

The **scope** of a variable means those parts of the code which can read or change its value. A variable's scope depends upon how and where it was created.

Global variables

Variables declared by assignment in the <BODY > of a document have **global scope**. They can be accessed by any JavaScript anywhere else in the document – in another <SCRIPT> block, in some event code, or in a <HEAD> function. They can even be accessed from other documents by prefacing the variable's name with the document's name. If you had a variable called *visitor* in a window called *mainWindow*, you could refer to it from another window by the name *mainWindow.visitor*.

Local variables

Variables declared by assignment in a function are local to that function. They cannot be accessed from any other code.

Variables declared with a *var* in a function are also local to the function. Use this format if there is another variable of the same name elsewhere in the document. It ensures that the one in the function is a separate, local, variable, and that the global one will still have the same value after the function has been executed.

The following example demonstrates the scope of variables. Two variables, *x* and *y*, are created by assigning values at the start of the BODY script. The values are displayed.

The function *dostuff()* is then called. Here, *x* is assigned a new value, but *y* is declared with a var and then assigned a new value. These values are displayed from within the function.

On return to the BODY script, the values are displayed one last time. *x* now holds the value assigned to it in the function, but *y* still holds its original value. This is because the *y* variable in the function was a separate, local, entity as it had been declared with a var. Whatever is done to the *y* in *dostuff()* has no effect on the *y* in the main script.

```
<HTML>
<HEAD>
<TITLE>Variables</TITLE>
<SCRIPT>
function dostuff()
{
    x = -1
    var y = 0
    document.write("<P>In the function x holds " + x + "
        and y holds " + y)
}
</SCRIPT>
```

```
</HEAD>
<BODY>
<SCRIPT>
   x = 99
   y = 1066
   document.write("Variable x holds " + x)
   document.write("<P>Variable y holds " + y)
   dostuff()
   document.write("<P>Back in the body, x has been
      changed to " + x + " but y still holds " + y)
</SCRIPT>
</BODY>
</HTML>
```

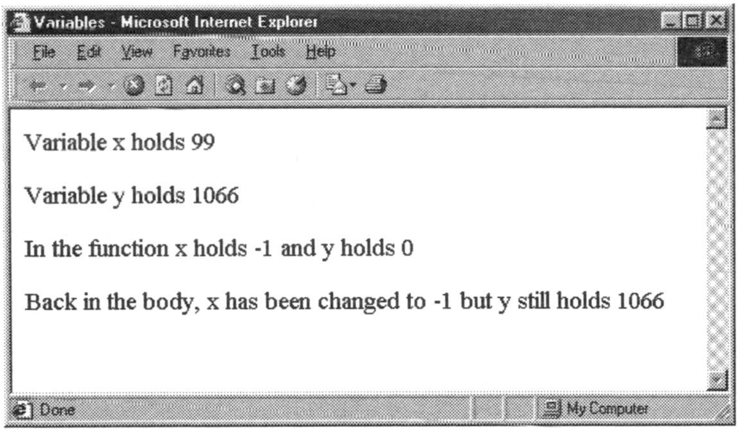

Variables - Microsoft Internet Explorer

File Edit View Favorites Tools Help

Variable x holds 99

Variable y holds 1066

In the function x holds -1 and y holds 0

Back in the body, x has been changed to -1 but y still holds 1066

Done — My Computer

Figure 3.1 The output. Experiment with the code. Does it make any difference if var is used when creating variables in the body?

Calculations

In JavaScript there are five arithmetic operators:

- + addition
- – subtraction
- * multiplication
- / division
- % modulus

The first four are used in exactly the same way as in normal arithmetic. The modulus operator gives you the remainder from integer division, e.g.

14 % 4 = 2

i.e. 14 divided by 4 produces 3, with a remainder of 2.

The values produced by arithmetic expressions can be used wherever you can use a variable or a literal value. You can write them on the screen, assign them to variables, or use them within other calculations. We'll start by printing them on the screen. This example displays the sums (as text) followed by the expressions. The system will calculate the results and display them.

```
<HTML>
<BODY>
<SCRIPT>
 document.write("42 + 5 = " + (42 + 5) + "<P>")
 document.write("42 - 5 = " + (42 - 5) + "<P>")
 document.write("42 * 5 = " + (42 * 5) + "<P>")
 document.write("42 / 5 = " + (42 / 5) + "<P>")
 document.write("42 % 5 = " + (42 % 5) + "<P>")
</SCRIPT>
</BODY>
</HTML>
```

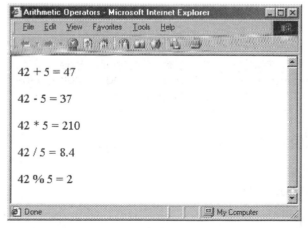

Figure 3.2 Numbers and operators written in quotes are treated as text; written in brackets they are treated as calculations. What happens if you miss out the brackets? Read on...

Number values and digits

When JavaScript sees a number, it can treat it either as a digit – i.e. as text – or as a value. If it is in quotes, it is definitely treated as text. If it is a number by itself, it is also treated as text. If it is in a calculation, JavaScript will usually recognize it as such, but may get it wrong. Look at this line:

```
document.write("42 + 5 =  " + 42 + 5 )
```

This will display:

```
42 + 5 = 425
```

Why? Because the + operator has two meanings – it can also be used to combine strings of text or mixed text and numbers. JavaScript treats the numbers in that line as if they were in quotes, like this:

```
document.write("42 + 5 =  " + "42" + "5" )
```

And so joins them together instead of adding them up.

Minus signs can also throw JavaScript.

```
document.write("42 + 5 =  " + 42 - 5 )
```

This will display **NaN**, which means Not a Number.

The solution is to put brackets around the calculations. This forces JavaScript to work out the calculation – so that you have a single number – before writing anything on screen.

Remove the brackets in the example on page 37 and see the effect.

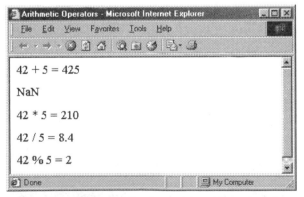

Figure 3.3 The same expressions, but without brackets.

Assignment operators

These combine an arithmetic operator with assignment (=), producing a shortcut for changing the value of a variable. But note that you can only use them where the same variable would appear on both sides. They look like this:

```
+=   –=   *=   /=   %=
```

and are used like this:

```
total += vat

num *= 2
```

These are the same as:

```
total = total + vat

num = num * 2
```

The += operator also works with text. For example:

```
username = "Jo"
username += " Bloggs"
```

username now holds "Jo Bloggs".

Increment and decrement

There are two other arithmetic operators. ++ (increment) and -- (decrement) will increase or decrease the value of a variable by 1. They are used like this:

```
num++
```

is quicker to type but has the same effect as:

```
num = num + 1
```

The operators can be used written before (*prefix*) or after (*postfix*) the variable name. If all you are doing is changing the value of that variable, it doesn't matter which form you use. These are identical:

```
num++
```

```
++num
```

If you are assigning the value to another variable or are displaying the value at the same time, the position of the operator is crucial.

    num2 = num1++

assigns the initial value of *num1* to *num2*, then increments *num1*.

    num2 = ++num1

increments *num1* before assigning its value to *num2*.

You can see this at work in the next example.

```
<HTML>
<BODY>
<SCRIPT>
    var count = 0
    document.write(count + "<P>")
    count++
    document.write("Incremented " + count + "<P>")
    document.write("Increment after " + count++ + "<P>")
    document.write("Increment before " + ++count + "<P>")
</SCRIPT>
</BODY>
</HTML>
```

Type it in and view the output. See what happens if you swap over the **Increment before...** and **Increment after...** lines. Try replacing the initial **count++** with **++count**.

Operator precedence

The calculations so far have been simple ones, with only one operator. You can have Java expressions with several operators and values – just as you can on paper. The rules of precedence apply here, much as in ordinary arithmetic.

Where there are several operators, multiplication and division are done first, then addition and subtraction, and finally the assignment operators (though these are normally used only in simple calculations).

If part of the expression is enclosed in brackets, that part is evaluated before the rest, e.g.:

```
2 + 3 * 4 – (9 – 3) / 2
```

This first has its bracketed operation solved to give:

```
2 + 3 * 4 – 6 / 2
```

then its multiplication and division:

```
2 + 12 – 3
```

and finally the addition and subtraction to produce 11.

Where you have a sequence of multiplication and division (or addition and subtraction), it does not matter which you do first, e.g.:

```
4 * 6/3   =  24/3 = 8
or        =  4 * 2 = 8
```

Bitwise operators

JavaScript also has bitwise operators. These see a number as a set of bits, e.g. 42 would be seen as 00101010, and can change the values of individual bits within a byte. They are mainly used for manipulating memory and input/output streams, and we don't have room for them in this book.

Arrays

Arrays let you store and manipulate information in bulk. Use them wherever you have a lot of related data, such as lists of names or URLs, sets of co-ordinates and the like.

The basic concepts of arrays are simple. Instead of having 10, 100, 1000 or more variables each with a unique name, you have one name which refers to the whole set, with each element identified by its *subscript* – its position in the set. The subscript is written in [square brackets] after the array name.

Array	Memory
nickname[0]	Doc
nickname[1]	Sneezy
nickname[2]	Happy

As the subscript can be a variable, you have a simple way of accessing any or all the elements in the array. We will look at this properly in the next chapter when we get on to ways of repeating actions, but here's a simple example to show what is possible. Suppose you had an array of 1000 numbers (*num*) and a variable (*count*). If you ran *count* through the full range of subscripts, while repeating this single line:

```
document.write(num[count]);
```

it would display all the numbers in the array.

If those numbers had been stored in individual variables, you would have needed 1000 writes to display them! You can see this in the next example. With only 8 elements, the effect is less dramatic, but the convenience of arrays is clearly visible.

Initializing arrays

An array is not a type of variable, as it is in other languages, but an object. To create an array, you use a line like this:

```
product = new Array(10)
```

This sets up an array, called *product*. The **new** constructor (the method that creates objects) allocates memory space for the array's elements.

Numbering starts from 0, so the subscripts for the elements in this array will run from *product[0]* to *product[9]*. Remember – [square brackets] around the subscripts, and subscripts can be literal values or variables.

The data stored in any single array must be of the same type, but it can be numbers, strings, images, buttons or other elements on forms.

Values are assigned to array elements in exactly the same way as they are to ordinary variables:

```
product[0] = "Widget, small"
product[1] = "Widget, medium"
```

And array elements are used in the same way in expressions and methods.

```
document.write("You have chosen " + product[choice])
```

Array methods

The Array object has several predefined methods which you can use on your new arrays.

join()   combines all the elements of an array into one string. This can then be output by giving the array name:

document.write("We sell: " + products)

reverse() turns the array on its head, so that it starts with its last element and finishes with its first

sort()   sorts the array into order. This is normally ascending alphabetical order though you can set it to sort descending, or numerically up or down.

To use one of these methods, simply tack its name to the name of the array. So, to sort the *products* array, you would use:

products.sort()

This next example creates an array of seven elements and stores in it some names. It then outputs them in their original order, and again as a sorted list. Feel free to replace my data with something of your own!

```
<HTML>
<BODY>
<SCRIPT>
   nickname = new Array(7)
   nickname[0] = "Doc"
   nickname[1] = "Sneezy"
   nickname[2] = "Happy"
   nickname[3] = "Sleepy"
   nickname[4] = "Dopey"
   nickname[5] = "Grumpy"
   nickname[6] = "Bashful"
   document.write("The names in the array: <BR>")
   for (dwarf = 0 ; dwarf < 7; dwarf++)
      document.write(nickname[dwarf] + "<BR>")
   nickname.sort()
   document.write("<P>The sorted list: <BR>")
   for (dwarf = 0; dwarf < 7; dwarf++)
      document.write(nickname[dwarf] + "<BR>")
   nickname.reverse()
```

```
        document.write("<P>And back the other way: <BR>")
        for (dwarf = 0; dwarf < 7; dwarf++)
            document.write(nickname[dwarf] + "<BR>")
        nickname.join()
        document.write("<P>All together now:" + nickname)
    </SCRIPT>
    </BODY>
    </HTML>
```

Notice the statement that is used to run through the list:

```
for (dwarf = 0; dwarf < 7; dwarf++)
    document.write(nickname[dwarf] + "<BR>")
```

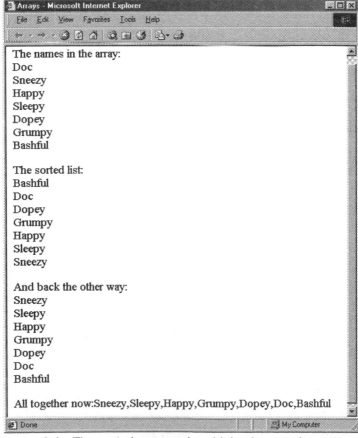

Figure 3.4 The sorted, reversed and joined array elements.

This sets *dwarf* to the values 0 to 6 in turn, repeating the following line with each value. We will look at **for** loops properly in the next chapter.

Exercises

1   Write code that assigns number values to two variables, then adds them together and assigns the result to a third variable and displays this with a write(). Edit the code to change the operation to subtraction and run it again. Repeat for the other operators.

2   Write code to work out this calculation:

$$\frac{10 + 6}{4} \times \frac{10 - 4}{3}$$

3   In that seven dwarves example, what is the state of the array after the join()? How can you check?

Summary

♦   Variables are named places in memory where you can store the data for use in programs.

♦   When naming variables, the most important rule is that the names must mean something to you!

♦   The **scope** of a variable depends mainly upon whereabouts it was created.

♦   JavaScript has five arithmetic operators: + (add), – (subtract), * (multiply), / (divide) and % (modulus).

♦   You can combine the assignment and arithmetic operators, to do the two operations at once.

♦   You can add or subtract 1 to a variable with the ++ (increment) and -- (decrement) operators.

♦   An array is a set of variables which all have the same name, and are identified by their subscript numbers. An array can be run through a loop to process data in bulk.

04 program flow

In this chapter you will learn

- how to compare values
- how to use loops to repeat blocks of code
- about branching programs with if and switch
- how to redirect program flow

Controlling programs

Program flow refers to the order in which instructions are carried out. So far, most of the example programs have run straight through a sequence, then stopped. There is a limit to what you can achieve with such simple programs. The use of loops and branches makes programs far more powerful.

* **Loops** repeat a set of instructions a fixed number of times or until a condition is met.

* **Branches** take the flow off down different routes, depending upon the values held by variables.

Before you can do much with either loops or branches, you need to know how to test the values in variables.

Comparison operators

These are used to compare the contents of variables with values or with the contents of other variables. There are six comparison operators:

==	equal to	!=	not equal to
<	less than	<=	less than or equal to
>	greater than	>=	greater than or equal to

Notice that the equality test uses a double equals sign '=='. The single sign '=' is used for assigning values.

Tests are enclosed in brackets, and typically look like this:

```
(x < 99)
(newNum != oldNum)
```

A test produces a Boolean value – *true* or *false*. Most of the time you do not need to worry about this – just use the test – but sometimes it is useful to store the result of the test in a variable, for reference later in the program, e.g.

```
result = (newNum > oldNum)
// store the test result
...
if (result == true)
// the same as using "if (newNum > oldNum)"
```

When testing to see if a Boolean value is true, you can miss out the '== true' part of the test, and it still works.

```
if (result)
```

is the same as

```
if (result == true)
```

Including '== true' can make the test a little more readable, but the shortform does make for neater expressions where you are testing several values at once – see below.

Logical operators

The comparison operators only test variables against one value at a time. Sometimes you want to check if a variable falls into a range of values, or is one of several possibilities. This is where the *logical operators* come into play.

AND

The && (AND) operator compares the results from two tests, with the expression being true if both tests are true.

```
( (x >= 20) && (x <= 30) )
```

This expression is true for all values of x from 20 to 30.

OR

With an || (OR) operator, the expression is true if either or both of the tests are true.

```
( (x > 100) || (y > 200) )
```

This expression is true if x is greater than 100 or y is greater than 200, or if both are over their limits.

A logical expression can have more than two tests and can include both && and ||.

In mixed expressions, && is evaluated first, unless you use brackets – as in arithmetic, anything in brackets is evaluated first.

```
( (x >= 20) && (x <= 30) || (y > 200))
```

For this to be true, the *x* value must be between 20 and 30, or the *y* value over 200 – in which case, the *x* value is irrelevant.

```
( ( (x > 100) || (y > 200) )  && (edgecheck) )
```

This is true if either, or both, the *x* and *y* values are over the limit, and if the Boolean variable *edgecheck* has been set to true.

for loops

A **for** loop allows you to repeat a set of instructions for a controlled number of times. The basic shape of the loop is:

```
for (var = start_value; end_test; change)
{
    statement(s);
}
```

When the program reaches this line for the first time, *var* is assigned its *start_value*. The *statement*, or block of statements, are executed, and the flow loops back to the **for** line. The value of *var* is then adjusted as specified by the *change* expression and the *end_test* is performed. This will normally compare *var* with a value, e.g. *counter < 100*. If the *end_test* is not met, the statements are performed again, and the flow continues to loop back until it is met.

The simplest type of **for** line has this shape:

```
for (counter = 0; counter <10; counter++)
```

This sets up a loop that will repeat its statements a total of 10 times, as *counter* is incremented through the values 0 to 9.

You can count in either direction. Try this:

```
<HTML>
<BODY>
<SCRIPT>
for (count = 10; count >=0; count--)
    document.write(count + "<BR>")
document.write("Blast off!!!")
</SCRIPT>
</BODY>
</HTML>
```

The increment and decrement operators give you neat ways to count up or down by 1 at a time, but you can take bigger steps. This loop will repeat 20 times, as *counter* is taken through the values 100, 95, 90, down to 0.

```
for (counter = 100; counter >0 ; counter -= 5)
```

The loop in this next example produces a simple times table display. Take care with the write() line – it is a bit complicated! Try it, then experiment with different start values, end tests and changes in the **for** settings.

```
<HTML>
<HEAD>
<TITLE>For loops: 2</TITLE>
</HEAD>
<BODY>
<SCRIPT>
    multiple = 6
    for (num = 1 ; num <=10; num++)
        document.write(num + " x " + multiple + " = " +
            (num * multiple) + "<BR>")
</SCRIPT>
</BODY>
</HTML>
```

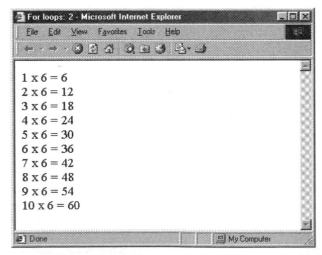

Figure 4.1 With a **for** loop you can easily run a block of code through a range of values.

Blocks of code

If you want to loop through a set of instructions, not just one, enclose the statements in {curly brackets}. This next example has three statements in the loop. The first writes the current value of *num*; the second adds it to *total*; the third displays *total* with a little text.

Two minor points to notice here:

+ The three statements in the loop have been indented a tab space. This helps to identify them as being a block.

+ There are spaces at either end of the text in the last write(). Why?

```
<HTML>
<BODY>
<SCRIPT>
   total = 0
   for (num = 1 ; num <=6; num++)
   {
      document.write(num)
      total += num
      document.write(" Total so far is " + total + "<BR>")
   }
</SCRIPT>
</BODY>
</HTML>
```

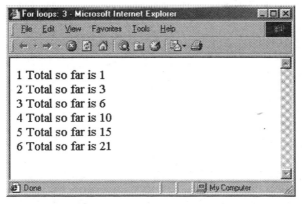

Figure 4.2 The output.

Varying loop values

The number of times that a for loop is repeated is determined by the start and end values and the rate of change, but these do not have to be fixed at design time. If any of these values are held in variables, they can be assigned by the program's user or calculated during its run.

In the next example, you decide the values by typing them into a form. The loop will then run to your specifications. *Do make sure that the loop can end!* If you set the change to 0, or the end value to less than the start (unless you want to count backwards), the browser will get stuck in an endless loop. The only way out of that will be to use [Ctrl]+[Alt]+[Delete] and end the program.

Notice how values are extracted from the text boxes:

```
start = eval(form1.startval.value)
```

startval is the name of the text box on *form1*. Its *value* – whatever is written in the box – is in fact text. To convert this to a number value, we use the **eval**() function. We will have a closer look at this on page 85. For the moment it is enough to know that it is necessary.

```
<HTML>
<HEAD>
<TITLE>For loops</TITLE>
<SCRIPT>
function doloop()
{
    start = eval(form1.startval.value)
    end = eval(form1.endval.value)
    change = eval(form1.changeval.value)
    for (num = start; num <=  end ; num += change)
        document.write(num + "  ")
    document.write("<P>Click the Back button to repeat")
}
</SCRIPT>
</HEAD>
<BODY>
<FORM NAME = form1>
Start value: <INPUT TYPE = text NAME = startval VALUE = 1>
```

```
<BR>
End value: <INPUT TYPE = text NAME = endval VALUE = 10>
<BR>
Change amount: <INPUT TYPE = text NAME = changeval
VALUE = 1>
<BR>
<INPUT TYPE = button VALUE = "Run the loop" onClick =
"doloop()">
</FORM>
</BODY>
</HTML>
```

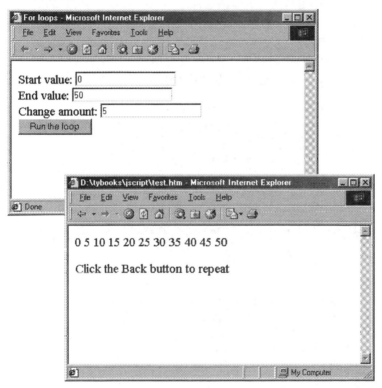

Figure 4.3 The form and the page produced by the script. The Change value can be negative, but if you want to count backwards, the end value must obviously be less than the start.

Nested loops

Loops can be 'nested' inside one another, with the inner loop running its full course each time the program flow passes through the outer loop. It's a technique that you might use to read an array, or to create a table of two (or more) dimensions.

The next example displays a 10 × 10 block of numbers, running 1 to 10 across the top and 1 to 10 down the left, with their multiples where the rows and columns meet. When you think that each of the loops could have a far higher end value, you realize just how much work you can get out of two or three lines of code, thanks to loops!

```
<HTML>
<BODY>
<SCRIPT>
for (row = 1; row <= 10 ; row++)
{
    for (col = 1; col <= 10 ; col++)
        document.write((row * col) + " ... ")
        // end of col loop
    document.write("<BR>")
}
</SCRIPT>
</HTML>
```

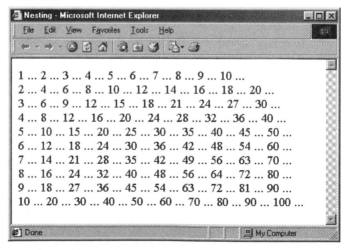

Figure 4.4 A times table produced from two nested loops.

The display could be neater! The problem is that the output from write() is HTML code, and HTML does not support tabs or display more than one space between items. Using dots for spacing us a crude solution, but we can have a nicely laid out table with a little effort – as you are about to see.

Tables from loops

Remember that you can **write** any HTML tags. If we want a neat table in HTML, we use <TABLE> tags. The key ones are the row <TR> and column <TD> tags, which will fit nicely into an inner and outer loop pattern.

We write a <TR> at the start of each row:

```
for (row = 1; row <= 10 ; row++) {
    document.write("<TR>")
```

and wrap each column entry in <TD> </TD> tags:

```
for (col = 1; col <= 10 ; col++)
    document.write("<TD>" + (row * col) + "</TD>")
```

The amount of space beween items, the border size and other options can be set as usual in the <TABLE> tag, written at the start, before the loops.

```
<HTML>
<BODY>
<SCRIPT>
document.write("<TABLE BORDER = 2 CELLSPACING =5
ALIGN = CENTER>")
for (row = 1; row <= 10 ; row++)
{
    document.write("<TR>")
    for (col = 1; col <= 10 ; col++)
        document.write("<TD>" + (row * col) + "</TD>")
        // end of inner (col) loop
    document.write("</TR>")
}
document.write("</TABLE>")
</SCRIPT>
</HTML>
```

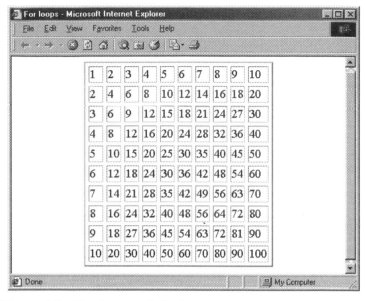

Figure 4.5 The improved display.

Dialog boxes

Before we go any further on ways to control program flow, let's have a look at dialog boxes. They offer a simple way to get values into a program, and that can be very useful for testing branching structures.

JavaScript has three ready-made dialog boxes that you can use to interact with your visitors. All three display a (fixed) title and a message, and halt the script until the user responds. The message can be text, or any expression that produces text.

• **alert(message)** carries only an **OK** button. Use it to let your visitors know that something has happened or is about to take place.

> alert("Your order has been processed")

* **confirm(message)** carries an **OK** and a **Cancel** button, and returns the Boolean values *true* or *false*, depending upon which button was clicked (**OK** returns *true*). Use it where you are offering your visitor a simple Yes/No choice.

  The reply should be assigned to a variable.

  ```
  doit = confirm("Do you really want to unsubscribe?")
  ```

* **prompt(message, default)** carries a text box and the **OK** and **Cancel** buttons. It returns whatever text was entered. Use it to get information on pages where there is no form. You can set a default value or use "" to clear the box. If you do not set a default, the text box displays 'undefined'.

  To capture the entered text, assign the **prompt()** to a variable:

  ```
  ccnum = prompt("Enter your Credit Card number","")
  ```

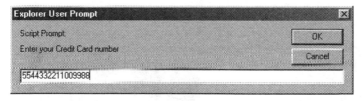

You can now use *ccnum* elsewhere in the code.

The data from a **prompt** is always text. If you need it to be a number value, use the eval() function like this:

```
num = eval(prompt("How many?",""))
```

We will return to **eval()** on page 85.

Look out for dialog boxes in the later programs in this chapter.

while loops

A **for** loop is normally repeated for a set number of times. A **while** loop gives you greater flexibility in two ways:

- the exit test is at the start of the loop – it is performed on entry and before each repetition. If the condition is met at the start, the loop's statements are not executed at all.

- the exit test can check the status of *any* variable, not just a loop counter.

The basic **while** loop takes this shape:

```
while (test)
   { statement(s) }
```

But there is actually more to it than that. The variable that is being tested must be given a value, somehow, sometime earlier, and it must be changed by some activity inside the loop.

Here a counter is used to determine the number of repetitions.

```
<HTML>
<BODY>
<SCRIPT>
   count = 0
   while (count < 10)
   {
      count++
      document.write("<BR>Count = " + count)
   }
</SCRIPT>
</HTML>
```

One of the things to notice here is that this displays 1 to 10, even though the text is **count < 10**. That's because count is incremented *after* the test and before it is printed. Change the order of the increment and print lines to this...

```
while (count < 10)
{
   document.write("<BR>Count = " + count)
   count++
}
```

... and you will get a 0 to 9 display. Watch out for this.

do...while

This variation on the **while** loop performs its test after the enclosed statements. The basic shape is:

```
do
{
    statement(s)
} while (test)
```

The statements will always be executed at least once before the test is performed, and will be repeated until the test proves false. A typical use would be where the repetition depends on user input or some other activity within the loop.

```
<HTML>
<BODY>
<SCRIPT>
    total = 0
    do
    {
        num = eval(prompt("How many?",""))
        total += num
        document.write("<BR>Total so far = " + total)
    }
    while (total < 100)
</SCRIPT>
</HTML>
```

Branching with if

Branches make programs flexible, allowing them to vary their actions in response to incoming data. The simplest form of branch uses the **if** structure. This is the basic syntax:

```
if (test)
    { statement(s) if true }
```

The *test* checks the value held by a variable. If the test proves true, the program performs the statement(s), otherwise they are ignored. For example:

```
if (balance < 0)
    alert("You are overdrawn")
```

The overdraft warning is only issued if the user has a balance below 0. Notice that as there was just the one statement, curly brackets were not needed.

You can see the **if** structure at work in the next example. First the script generates a random number, with this line:

```
x = Math.round(Math.random()*100)
```

This uses two Math methods, **round**() and **random**(). They are explained properly in Chapter 5, pages 82 and 83 – for the moment, please just accept that the line works and that it will produce a whole number in the range 0 to 99.

The code then gets the computer to work out the value of a random number, which it does by splitting the difference between the highest and lowest possible values. If its 'guess' is too high, or too low, a message is displayed and the upper or lower limits adjusted.

The **round**() method is used again later in the line which calculates *guess*. It rounds the result up to the next whole number.

```
guess = Math.round((max + min) / 2)
```

The program runs through a **while** loop, which tests the guess against the random number. The initial guess is 50. How does that relate to the line which calculates the next value of *guess*?

```
<HTML>
<BODY>
<SCRIPT>
    x = Math.round(Math.random()*100)
    max = 100
    min = 0
    count = 0
    guess = 50
    while (guess != x)
    {
        document.write("<BR>Trying " + guess)
        count++
        if (guess > x)
        {
            document.write(" Too high")
            max = guess
        }
```

```
    if (guess < x)
    {
        document.write(" Too low")
        min = guess
    }
    guess = Math.round((max + min) / 2)
}
    document.write("<P>It was " + guess)
    document.write("<BR> Found it in " + count + " goes.")
</SCRIPT>
</HTML>
```

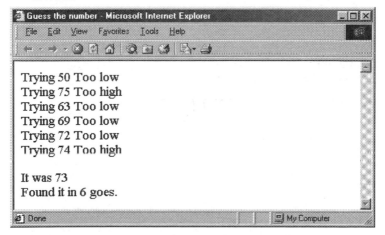

Figure 4.6 A typical output – the computer never takes more than seven goes. Why not?

if ... else

This variation on the **if** structure uses the **else** keyword, which handles the actions to perform if the test does *not* prove true. The syntax is:

```
if (test)
    { statement(s) if true}
else
    { statement(s) if false}
```

For example:

```
if (total > 100)
    carriage = 2.00
else
    carriage = 5.00
```

The carriage charge is £2.00 if you spend over £100, otherwise it is £5.00.

The basic **if** structure has the beauty of simplicity – it shows clearly the relationship between the test and the outcome. But it is not always the best solution. Consider this problem. You want to analyse a character to see if it is an upper or lower case letter, digit or a symbol. Here's the first draft of a program to do the job.

```
<HTML>
<HEAD>
<TITLE>Character tester</TITLE>
</HEAD>
<BODY>
<SCRIPT>
    letter = prompt("Enter a character"," ")
    while (letter != "q")
    {
        if (letter < " ")
            alert("Non-printing character entered")
        if (letter >= "a" && letter <= "z")
            alert("Lower case letter entered")
        if (letter >= "A" && letter <= "Z")
            alert("Upper case letter entered")
        if (letter >= "0" && letter <= "9")
            alert("Digit entered")
        letter = prompt("Enter a character - q to quit"," ")
    }
</SCRIPT>
</HTML>
```

So far, so good. The first test spots the non-printing characters (tab, carriage return, movement, etc. which are clustered at the start of the character set, ending at space). The next three tests handle the sets, 'a' to 'z', 'A' to 'Z' and '0' to '9'. What about the rest?

Look at any character set (use the Character Map in Windows Accessories), and you will see that there are punctuation and other symbols scattered between the blocks of letters and digits. A test for these would look like this:

```
if ((letter > " ") && (letter < "0") || (letter >= "9") && (letter <
    "A") || (letter > "Z") && (letter <= "a") || (letter >= "z"))
```

This is not an elegant solution! And it's not just that it doesn't look nice. Complicated code is more likely to contain errors. This expression took some time to work out and to test – and I'm still not 100% sure about it!

Here's a much better solution. The **if ... else** structure gives two branches from the same test – one to follow if it is true, and one if it is false. This can be extended to handle multiple branching.

```
if (test1)
    {statement(s) if test1 is true}
else if (test2)
    {statement(s) if test2 is true}
else
    {statement(s) if no tests are true}
```

If *test1* is false, the program tries *test2*, and failing that, tries the next. If all the tests prove false, the program performs the statements after the final **else**. Here's the revised routine.

```
<HTML>
<HEAD>
<TITLE>Character tester</TITLE>
</HEAD>
<BODY>
<SCRIPT>
    letter = prompt("Enter a character"," ")
    while (letter != "q")
    {
        if (letter < " ")
            alert("Non-printing character entered")
        else if (letter >= "a" && letter <= "z")
            alert("Lower case letter entered")
        else if (letter >= "A" && letter <= "Z")
            alert("Upper case letter entered")
```

```
            else if (letter >= "0" && letter <= "9")
                alert("Digit entered")
            else
                alert("Symbol entered")
            letter = prompt("Enter a character - q to quit"," ")
        }
    </SCRIPT>
    </HTML>
```

If a character is not picked up by any of the tests, the **else** statement is performed, and the "Symbol entered" message displayed.

Three minor points to note here.

+ This shows the use of a **prompt** dialog box to get input, and an **alert** to display messages.

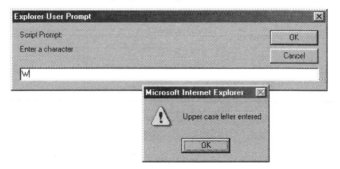

+ There are lines prompting the user for a character before the **while** line and again at the end of the loop. The **while** needs something to test when it first starts.

+ Where you have a series of separate **if** statements, the program will check each one, even after it has had a true result. With a compound **if ... else if ... else** structure like this, the program flow will jump to the end once it has found a match. If the testing was being done repeatedly while processing a mass of data there could be an appreciable improvement in running speed.

switch

The **switch** structure can be used to replace a whole set of **if** statements, where these all test the same simple variable for different values. A typical use would be with a menu, where the switch directs the flow to the chosen option's routine. The basic shape of the structure is:

```
switch (expression)
{                                          Alternative layouts
    case value:
        statement(s)
        break
    case value: statement(s); break
    ...
    default :  statement(s)
}
```

◆ The switch does a simple match, comparing each of the *values* with the *expression* – you cannot use the relational operators here.

◆ The values must be enclosed in quotes and followed by a colon.

◆ You need a **break** at the end of each of the case statements to jump out of the switch block.

◆ The statements can be written on a series of lines or on a single line. In the latter case they must be separated by semicolons.

◆ The statements on the (optional) **default** line are performed if there are no matching cases.

◆ You can only test one value with each **case**. If several values lead to the same actions, write them on successive lines. e.g.:

```
case "purple" :
    case "pink" :
        document.write("Wazzup? You colour blind?")
```

The following program shows **switch** at work. Notice this line:

```
colour =colour. toLowerCase()
```

This uses the String function **toLowerCase**() to convert whatever the user enters into lower case, making it simpler to check.

```
<HTML>
<BODY>
<SCRIPT>
    colour = prompt("What is your favourite colour?","")
    colour =colour. toLowerCase()
    switch (colour) {
        case "red" :
            document.write("You have a passionate nature")
            break
        case "blue" :
            document.write("You tend to be cool and calm")
            break
        case "green" :
            document.write("You are at one with nature")
            break
        case "purple" :
        case "pink" :
            document.write("Wazzup? You colour blind?")
            break
        default : document.write("That's a very nice colour")
    }
</SCRIPT>
</HTML>
```

The conditional operator

The conditional operator ? : is a shortform of **if ... else**. It can be used for assigning alternative values based on a test, though not for redirecting program flow. It can be convenient, though what you gain in compactness you lose in readability.

The basic shape is:

```
variable = (test ? value_if_true : value_if_false)
```

Here's a simple example of its use. This gives a 10% discount if the total is more than £250:

```
discount = ( total > 250 ? 0.10 : 0)
```

The equivalent **if ... else** would be:

```
if (total > 250)
    discount = 0.1
else
    discount = 0
```

It is often used within a larger expression. For example, this firm charges £10 for delivery for orders under £100, and £5 where the total is more. The line to calculate the cost is:

```
cost = total + (total < 100 ? 5 : 0)
```

Using **if ... else**, the code would be:

```
if (total < 100)
    cost = total + 5
else
    cost = total
```

You can see the conditional operator at work in this example. When you run it, enter values below 100, between 100 and 250 and above 250, to check that both operators work properly. (Reload the page after each run to restart the program.)

```
<HTML>
<HEAD>
<TITLE>Conditional operator</TITLE>
</HEAD>
<BODY>
<SCRIPT>
    total = prompt("Enter total spent"," ")
    discount = (total > 250 ? total * 0.1 : 0)
    carriage = (total > 100 ? 5 : 10 )
    due = total - discount + carriage
    document.write("Total = " + total)
    document.write("<BR>Discount = " + discount)
    document.write("<BR>Carriage = " + carriage)
    document.write("<BR>Amount due = " + due)
</SCRIPT>
</HTML>
```

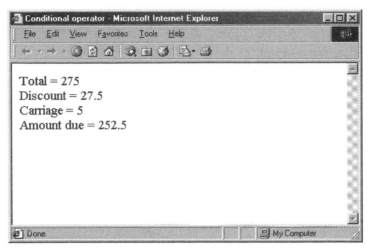

Figure 4.7 The display is not very tidy, and sometimes the discount value can run to 15 decimal places (try 267.67, for example). We'll think about making things look nice later.

label

A label does not actually do anything. Its purpose is to identify a place in the code so that program flow can be redirected to it by a **switch**, **break** or **continue** statement. The basic shape is:

label : *statement(s)*

label can be any word, following the same rules as for variable names, except for the JavaScript reserved words (see page 155). Note that they must be followed by a colon.

```
restart:
    document.write("Picking up again")
```

break

We saw **break** used with **switch** (page 65). It also provides a way of escaping from **for** or **while** loops. It is essential if there is a possibility that the exit condition will *never* be met, but it can also be useful where you just need an alternative exit.

In the example, the loop allows users three chances to work out the answer to a sum.

If they give the correct answer, the break forces an early exit from the loop. By checking the loop variable, *count*, after the end of the loop, the program can tell whether the user failed (count == 3) or got it right (early exit).

The values for *num1* and *num2* are random numbers generated by the Math methods, **round**() and **random**(). In this case, the values will be in the range 1 to 20.

```
<HTML>
<HEAD>
<TITLE>Breaking out of loops</TITLE>
</HEAD>
<BODY>
<SCRIPT>
    num1 = Math.round(Math.random()*20)
    num2 = Math.round(Math.random()*20)
    for(count = 0; count < 3; count++)
    {
        answer = prompt("What is " + num1 + " times  " +
        num2, " ")
        if (answer == num1 * num2)
            break
    }
    if (count == 3)
        alert("The answer was " + (num1 * num2))
    else
        alert("Well done")
</SCRIPT>
</HTML>
```

break to a label

If you have nested loops, they can be labelled, and the labels used to control the breaks. In the example below, there are two loops labelled *outer* and *inner* and controlled by variables *n* and *m*. The loops are both set up to count from 0 to 4, but are tested inside the inner loop. The crucial lines are:

```
if (m ==3) break inner
if (n == 2) break outer
```

When *m* reaches 3, the program breaks out of the *inner* loop; when *n* reaches 2, the program breaks out of the *outer* loop.

```
<HTML>
<BODY>
<SCRIPT>
    outer:
    for(n = 0; n < 5; n++)
        inner:
        for(m = 0; m < 5; m++)
        {
            if (m ==3) break inner
            if (n == 2) break outer
            document.write("n = " + n + " m = " + m + "<BR>")
        }
</SCRIPT>
</HTML>
```

The output should be:

```
n = 0 m = 0
n = 0 m = 1
n = 0 m = 2
n = 1 m = 0
n = 1 m = 1
n = 1 m = 2
```

What happens if you remove the labels from the breaks?

continue

continue is similar to **break**, but where **break** takes the flow right out of the loop, **continue** just skips any remaining lines and loops round again. Use it where the lines in the lower part of the loop should only be performed if a condition is met.

In this example, the user is asked for two numbers, and the program then divides the first by the second. As division by 0 cannot be done, the code uses **continue** to restart the loop if a 0 is entered.

```
<HTML>
<BODY>
<SCRIPT>
alert("Welcome to the divider")
num1 = 99
```

```
while (num1 != 0)
{
   num1 = prompt("Enter first number or 0 to exit"," ")
   if (num1 == 0)
      break
   num2 = prompt("Enter second number", " ")
   if (num2 == 0)
   {
      alert("Division by 0! Restart sum")
      continue
   }
   ans = num1 / num2
   alert(num1 + " divided by " +  num2 + " = " + ans )
}
</SCRIPT>
</HTML>
```

We could have used an **if ... else** structure to control the flow at the end of the loop:

```
if (num2 != 0)
{
   ans = num1 / num2
   alert(num1 + " divided by " +  num2 + " = " + ans)
}
else
   alert("Division by 0! Restart sum")
```

continue is neater where there are a lot of lines to jump over.

Division by 0

In most programming languages, an attempt to divide by 0 will cause the program to crash. JavaScript is more forgiving – it gives you 'infinity' as the result.

continue with labels

Labels can be used with **continue** in much the same way as they can with **break**. Here are the same nested loops, but this time the tests check whether the numbers are even or odd (% performs modulus division, giving the remainder – if you can divide by 2 with no remainder, the number is even):

```
if (m%2 == 1) continue inner
if (n%2 == 0) continue outer
```

If the inner counter, *m*, is odd, the program will skip over the write line and start the next inner loop. If the outer counter, n, is even, the program will skip back to the start of the next outer loop. Here's the program. Apart from the **if...** lines it is the same as the break with labels example.

```
<HTML>
<BODY>
<SCRIPT>
outer:
for(n = 0; n < 5; n++)
    inner:
    for(m = 0; m < 5; m++)
    {
        if (m%2 == 1) continue inner
        if (n%2 == 0) continue outer
            document.write("n = " + n + " m = " + m + "<BR>")
    }
</SCRIPT>
</HTML>
```

You should see this output:

```
n = 1 m = 0
n = 1 m = 2
n = 1 m = 4
n = 3 m = 0
n = 3 m = 2
n = 3 m = 4
```

Error handling

JavaScript is a tolerant language. Once you have got code working, there is nothing much that can go wrong. As long as you avoid letting a program slip into an endless loop, the worst that happens is that nothing happens!

If, when you have finished working through this introductory book you want to get deeper into JavaScript – and particularly if you want to start using server-side JavaScript, look up the **try...catch** structure in the JavaScript Reference. This can capture errors before they crash your program.

Exercises

1 Using nested **for** loops, produce a display like this.

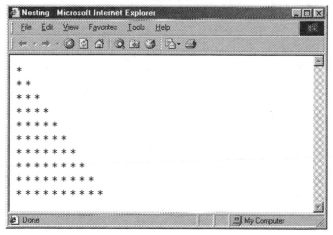

2 Using a **while** loop, count from 10 down to 0 on screen, ending with a message announcing a successful launch.

3 Rewrite the guessing program on page 60 to make it interactive. Use a prompt to collect guesses from the user.

4 A club has four categories and rates of membership: Standard, £50; Junior (16 and under), £10; Senior (65 and over), £15; Concession (unemployed), £20. Use prompts to collect the necessary data and display the category and rate.

Summary

- Program flow refers to the order in which instructions are carried out. It may be a simple sequence or flow through loops or branches.

- The comparison and logical operators are used to test values.

- A **for** loop counts its way round a block of code for a number of times, determined by the start value, end test and change.

- **for** loops can be nested inside one another.

- A **while** loop repeats a block of code until the exit condition is met.

- Dialog boxes offer a simple but effective way to interact with users.

- With **if** and **switch** structures, program flow depends upon the value held in variables.

- The conditional operator is a compact alternative to **if...else** for setting values.

- A **label** can be used to create a jump point in a program.

- You can force an early exit from a loop with **break** or **continue**.

05

functions and methods

In this chapter you will learn

- how to create functions and pass data to and from them
- about the Math methods
- how to read and display the date and time
- about manipulating text with the String methods

Functions

A function is a self-contained block of code, identified by a name. It may carry out some kind of calculation and return a value, or it may simply perform a task.

In most programming languages, functions are used to break a program down into manageable chunks – it's hard to read and debug a block of code larger than a page. In JavaScript, functions have another purpose. As they can be written into the <HEAD> area of a page, you can be sure that they are loaded and ready to run before the page begins to load. Where scripts are in the <BODY>, there is a danger that the browser will attempt to run them while they are still loading.

A function is *called* (activated) by giving its name in another line of code. After it has been executed, the program flow returns to the point in the code immediately after the call. The process can be taken further, with one function calling another, which calls another, and so on. When the program flow reaches the end of its current function, it returns to the function from which it was called, and so on back up to the main script.

Let's look at a simple example. First, let's take the program as one block of code. It works out the cube of a number, using a loop. To see how it works, 'dry run' the program on paper, writing down the values held by *ans* and *count* as the program runs through the loop:

```
<HTML>
<HEAD>
<TITLE>Calculating the cube</TITLE>
</HEAD>

<BODY>
<SCRIPT>
   num = 4
   ans = 1
   for (count = 1; count <= 3; count++)
      ans = ans * num;
      document.write(num + " ^ 3 = " + ans)
</SCRIPT>
</HTML>
```

Here's the same calculation, but performed through a function. In this version, both the calculation and the output lines have been transferred to the function.

```
<HTML>
<HEAD>
<TITLE>Cube as a function</TITLE>
<SCRIPT>
function cube(num)
{
    ans = 1
    for (count = 1; count <= 3; count++)
        ans = ans * num;
        document.write(num + " ^ 3 = " + ans + "<BR>")
}
// ^ means "to the power of"
</SCRIPT>
</HEAD>
<BODY>
<SCRIPT>
n =5
cube(n)
</SCRIPT>
</HTML>
```

Notice the calling line in the BODY script...

```
cube(n)
```

... and the function's definition line:

```
function cube(num)
```

The variable *n* is assigned the value 5 in the BODY script, and is passed to the function in *cube(n)*. There it is picked up by the parameter *num*, which acts as a normal variable within *cube()*.

The choice of names is deliberate – the names of parameters can be the same as or different from those of the variables that are passed to them. The parameters and variables in *cube()* are completely separate from those in the BODY script. These lines would have worked just as well:

```
n =5
cube(n)
```

Parameters

When passing values to a function, you must pass the right type of data, though it can be either as a variable or a literal value. This call to *cube()* would also work:

```
cube(5)
```

Add that line to the BODY script, and run the program again. The output this time should be:

```
5 ^ 3 = 125
4 ^ 3 = 64
```

A function can take any number of parameters, and these can carry text or numbers. The next example has this function:

```
function greeting(text, times)
```

It writes the *text*, repeating it as many *times* as required. In the next script, you can see examples of data being passed both as variables…

```
greeting(words, repeat)
```

and as literal values:

```
greeting("Bye ", 2)
```

```
<HTML>
<HEAD>
<TITLE>Parameters</TITLE>
<SCRIPT>
function greeting(text, times)
{
    for (count = 1; count <= times; count++)
        document.write(text)
}
</SCRIPT>
</HEAD>

<BODY>
<SCRIPT>
words = "Hello "
repeat = 3
greeting(words, repeat)
```

```
document.write("<BR>")
greeting("Bye ", 2)
</SCRIPT>
</HTML>
```

You must pass the same number of values – and in the right order. This will not work:

```
greeting(3, "Hello")
```

Return values

You may recall, from your school mathematics, using cosines and other functions. These return values, which can be used wherever you would use an ordinary value, e.g.

```
x = cos(y)
```

or

```
adjacent = cos(angle) * hypotenuse
```

A JavaScript function can also return a value. To do this, use the keyword **return** followed by the value. The **return** line is normally the last line in the function. You could, for example, define a function *cube()* like this:

```
function cube(x)
{
    return x * x * x
}
```

Here's the cube program again, this time rewritten so that the *cube()* function returns the result to the calling code.

```
<HTML>
<HEAD>
<TITLE>Cube as a function - 2</TITLE>
<SCRIPT>
function cube(num)
{
    ans = 1
    for (count = 1; count <= 3; count++)
        ans = ans * num;
    return ans
}
```

```
</SCRIPT>
</HEAD>
<BODY>
<SCRIPT>
n =5
result = cube(n)
document.write(n + " ^ 3 = " + result)
</SCRIPT>
</HTML>
```

Notice the line that calls the function:

```
result = cube(n)
```

A simple *cube(n)* would not get the answer. Bearing in mind that a function that returns a value is treated as any other value, you could equally well call it from within the write() line:

```
document.write(n + " ^ 3 = " + cube(n))
```

A function can have several return lines. Here is a function, *compare()*, which tests two values and returns 1 if the first is larger, −1 if it is smaller or 0 if they are the same:

```
function compare(a,b)
{
    if (a > b)  return 1
    else if (a < b)  return -1
    else return 0
}
```

Recursion

Not only can a function call another function, it can also call itself. This is known as recursion. (Hence the famous computer dictionary definition '**recursion**: see *recursion*'.) It is similar to running code through a loop, and is useful when you need to analyse something into its components. But use with care. If you do not leave an escape route, the program will lock into an endless cycle.

Here's a simple example of a recursive function. This calculates factorial values. A factorial is a whole number that is multiplied by every number below it, down to 1. It is indicated by a shriek (!) after the number, e.g. 5!

Look at the start of the factorial sequence:

1! = 1			
2! = 2 × 1	or	2 × 1!	
3! = 3 × 2 × 1	or	3 × 2!	
4! = 4 × 3 × 2 × 1	or	4 × 3!	

You can find the factorial of any number by multiplying that number by the one factorial of the next lower number. This works all the way down to 1!, which is equal to 1. We can turn this into pseudo-code (i.e. written in English, but structured like code).

```
if the number is 1
    the factorial is 1
else
    the factorial is the number times the factorial of the
next lower number
```

Which translates directly to this function:

```
function factorial(num)
{
    if (num==1)
        return num
    else
        return num * factorial(num-1)
}
```

So, if you first call the function with the expression *factorial(3)*, it will produce the expression *3 * factorial(2)* – calling itself. On the next time round, it generates *2 * factorial(1)* and calls itself again. This time it gets the answer *1*, and returns this value to the previous call, which uses it to calculate the value *2*, returning that to the top level. At this point the function does *3 * 2* and gets the answer *6*, which it passes back to the calling script.

Type it in and test it. The script opens with a prompt so that you can enter any value you like. For the initial testing, use numbers that are small enough for you to be able to work out the answer yourself, then find out what 100! looks like!

```
<HTML>
<HEAD>
<TITLE>Factorial</TITLE>
<SCRIPT>
function factorial(num)
{
    if (num==1)
        return num
    else
        return num * factorial(num-1)
}
</SCRIPT>
</HEAD>
<BODY>
<SCRIPT>
n = prompt("Enter a number","")
document.write(n + "! = " + factorial(n))
</SCRIPT>
</HTML>
```

The Math methods

JavaScript has 20 mathematical methods. They all belong to the **Math** object, and the only reason why you need to know that is because it is part of the name of the methods. We used two of these **Math.round**() and **Math.random**() in Chapter 4 to produce random numbers. Let's have a closer look at them, and at the other methods.

Random numbers

Math.random( ) generates a random number in the range 0 to 1. Used at its simplest, e.g.

```
x = Math.random()
```

this will give you a value between 0.0 and 1.0. If you want a decent sized number, this must be mutiplied. Multiply by 10 to get a number in the range of 0 to 10 – but it will have a decimal fraction. This gives you a number between 0 and 1000.

```
x = Math.random() * 1000
```

The numbers produced by random() are not, strictly speaking random, but are created by a complex mathematical process. However, they can be treated as random if the numbers are unpredictable and each number in the range is as likely to come up as any other. This next example will test the random number generator. It produces 1000 random numbers, and checks each to see if it is above or below 0.5, keeping a count of the high and low values in the variables *over* and *under*. You should get around 500 of each.

```
<HTML>
<BODY>
<SCRIPT>
    over = 0
    under = 0
    for(count = 0; count <1000; count++)
    {
        x =Math.random()
        if (x<0.5)
            over = over + 1
        else
            under = under + 1
    }
    document.write("0 to 0.5 " + over + " over 0.5 " + under
        + "<BR>")
</SCRIPT>
</HTML>
```

Rounding

round() converts a decimal value up or down to the nearest integer, e.g.

```
Math.round(5.67) = 6
Math.round(5.43) = 5
```

There are two other methods for converting decimals to integers:

ceil(*num*) rounds *up* to the next integer

```
Math.ceil(5.5) = 6
```

floor(*num*) rounds *down* to the next integer.

```
Math.floor(5.5) = 5
```

Type in this code and run it a few times to see the difference between **round**(), **ceil**() and **floor**().

```
<HTML>
<BODY>
<SCRIPT>
   n=prompt("Enter a decimal number"," ")
   document.write("You entered " +n)
   document.write("<BR> round = "+ Math.round(n))
   document.write("<BR> ceil = "+ Math.ceil(n))
   document.write("<BR> floor = "+ Math.floor(n))
</SCRIPT>
</HTML>
```

You could apply one or other of these to your random numbers to turn them into integers, e.g.

```
x = Math.round(Math.random() * 10)
```

The question is, which one? Does it make any difference which rounding method you use. Here's some code to test it. Run it for a few times using **round**() and note the results, then repeat with **ceil**() and **floor**().

Notice this function in the HEAD:

```
function rand(size)
{
    return Math.round(Math.random() * size)
}
```

This allows us to use the simpler expression **rand(10)** in the BODY script. If you find that you need a complex expression in a script, it is often worth converting it into a separate function. It makes for a more readable script, and it will be simpler to edit the function if you need to adjust the expression.

```
<HTML>
<HEAD>
<SCRIPT>
function rand(size)
{
    return Math.round(Math.random() * size)

}
```

```
</SCRIPT>
</HEAD>
<BODY>
<SCRIPT>
store = new Array(11)
/* create an array numbered 0 to 10 */
for(loop = 0; loop <= 10; loop++)
    store[loop] = 0
for(count = 0; count <1000; count++)
{
    /* generate a random number in the range 0 to 10 */
    x =rand(10)
    /* increment the counter for that number */
    store[x] = store[x] + 1
}
for(loop = 0; loop <= 10; loop++)
    document.write("store["+loop + "] has " + store[loop] +
"<BR>")
</SCRIPT>
</HTML>
```

Strings and numbers

eval() will give you the numerical value of a string or the result of a calculation. Try this to see it at work:

```
<HTML>
<BODY>
<SCRIPT>
calcString = prompt("Enter a calculation","")
alert("The value is " + eval(calcString) )
</SCRIPT>
</HTML>
```

eval() recognizes the standard symbols and follows the normal rules of arithmetic. Enter '2 + 3 * 4' and you should get 14. Enter '(2 + 3) * 4' and you should get 20. Take the eval() out of the alert line and try again. What does this display?

```
alert("The value is " + calcString )
```

toString(*num*) converts a number to a string. Its main purpose is in tidying up the display of numbers. When you do calculations in JavaScript, you will sometimes get odd results. Instead of 4, say, you will be given 3.999999999 or 4.0000001. This is because the computer works in binary, and converts values to denary (normal numbers) for the screen. The conversion is not always perfect, and you may want to tidy it up. Where you want to display currency values, you will need to adjust them to 2 decimal places. There may be other values that you might want to pad out with leading 0s. There is not much you can do about the display of numbers as long as they are number values, but as strings they can be manipulated in a variety of ways. We will come back to this shortly when we look at the String methods.

Trigonometry

JavaScript has the standard trigonometry functions: **cos()**, **sin()** and **tan()** which give the sine, cosine and tangent of angles, and also has **acos()**, **asin()**, **atan()** and **atan2()** which convert sines, cosines and tangets back into angles.

The main thing to note here is that like most programming languages, JavaScript measures angles in *radians*, not in the *degrees* which are more familiar to most people.

A radian is the angle where the arc on the circumference is equal to the radius of the circle.

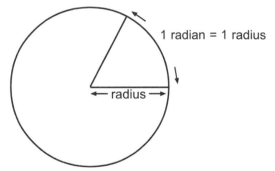

You should remember from your school maths that there are 2Pi radians in a circle (circumference = 2*Pi*radius). We can use this to work out the value of 1 radian:

1 radian = 360 / 2 * Pi degrees

= 180 / 3.14

= 57.3 degrees (approximately)

If you are happier working in degrees than in radians, these functions will convert the values for you.

```
function toDegree(radian)
    {
        return radian * 180 / Math.PI
    }

function toRadian(degree)
    {
        return degree * Math.PI / 180
    }
```

PI is a property of the Math object and has a value of 3.141592653589793 – which should be close enough for most purposes.

The trigonometry methods are covered in a little more detail in the Methods summary in Chapter 9, and you will see some of them in use in the JavaScript calculator on page 121.

Other Math methods

abs(*num*) gives you the absolute value of a number, i.e. it strips off the minus sign (if present), so that abs(-4) = abs(4) = 4. Here's a silly game which shows it at work.

```
<HTML>
<HEAD>
<TITLE>Absolutely wrong</TITLE>
</HEAD>
<BODY>
<SCRIPT>
    num = Math.round(Math.random() * 100)
    guess = prompt("What's my number?","")
    while (guess != num)
    {
        missedBy = Math.abs(guess - num)
        guess = prompt("Missed by " + missedBy + " Try
            again","")
    }
    alert("You got it!")
</SCRIPT>
</HTML>
```

pow(*n,p*) raises *n* to the power of *p* and **sqrt(*num*)** gives the square root of a number. You can see both of these in use in the JavaScript calculator (page 121).

max(*num1,num2*) returns the highest of two numbers.

```
top = max(num1,num2)
```

This is the same as the code:

```
if (num1> num2)
    top = num1
else top = num2
```

or even

```
top = (num1>num2? num1 : num2)
```

min(*num1,num2*) similarly returns the lowest of the two.

Finally, **log(*num*)** gives the logarithm of a number, and **exp(*log*)** converts a logarithm back into a number.

Date methods

If you want to do any work with dates or time, have a look at the **Date()** object and its methods. You can use it to:

- get the current date and time from your system's clock

- convert a date written in figures or in words and figures into a standard Date form

- set any part of the date, from year down to second

- calculate the elapsed time between two dates or times.

If you want to store dates, you must hold them in Date objects, not simple variables.

This line creates a Date object and sets it to the current date and time:

```
today = new Date( )
```

Notice the empty brackets at the end. If you want to set any other date when you create the object, write it in the brackets:

```
myParty = new Date("April 5th, 2003 19:30:00")
myParty  = new Date(2003, 4, 5, 19, 30, 0)
```

Where the date is written as text the whole expression must be enclosed in quotes. The last three figures – hours, minutes, seconds – are optional in both forms.

If you write the Date value or copy it to a text box, without processing it in any way, it will be displayed in the standard form. These lines:

```
today = new Date()
document.write(today)
```

produce output like this:

```
Thu Apr 10 10:28:06 UTC+0100 2003
```

This tells us the date and time, and the variation from the universal time clock (UTC), but it is not a display that you would normally want to use.

To improve the display, we first need to break the date information down into its components. The methods **getYear()**, **getMonth()**, **getDay()**, **getDate()**, **getHours()**, **getMinutes()** and **getSeconds()** will do this.

```
thisDay = today.getDay()
```

getDay() returns the *number* of the day of the week, counting from 0 on Sunday. If you want to display the day in words, you will have to set up an array, then draw the day out of it.

```
days = new Array("Sunday","Monday", "Tuesday",
"Wednesday", "Thursday", "Friday", "Saturday")
weekday = days[thisDay]
```

As I write this, *thisDay* is 4, and *weekday* is 'Thursday'.

The **getMonth()** method similarly gives you the month number, starting with January at 0. This gives you a simple translation if you set up an array of month names, but watch out for it if you want to display the month as a number – you must add 1.

This line – and notice the +1 after **getMonth()**...

```
document.write( today.getDate() + "/" + (today.getMonth()
+ 1) + "/" + today.getYear())
```

...displayed this on the 10th April:

```
10/4/2003
```

Here are some of the Date methods at work. Look for a version of this, and for a similar routine to handle months in the next example.

```
<HTML>
<HEAD>
<TITLE>Dates</TITLE>
</HEAD>
<BODY>
<SCRIPT>
/* set up arrays of day and month names */
days = new Array("Sunday","Monday", "Tuesday",
"Wednesday", "Thursday", "Friday", "Saturday")
months = new Array("Jan", "Feb", "March", "April", "May",
"June", "July", "Aug", "Sept", "Oct", "Nov", "Dec")

/* Get today's date, then extract the components */
today = new Date()
thisDay = today.getDay()
thisDate = today.getDate()
thisMonth = today.getMonth()
thisYear = today.getYear()

/* write the date in figures */
document.write( thisDate + "/" + (thisMonth + 1) + "/" +
thisYear + "<P>")

/* write the date in words and figures */
todayDay = days[thisDay]
todayMonth = months[thisMonth]
document.write( todayDay + ", " + todayMonth + " " +
thisDate + " " + thisYear)
</SCRIPT>
</BODY>
</HTML>
```

You should see something like this, but for the current date.

```
10/4/2003
Thursday, April 10 2003
```

Time

If you want to display the time, the technique is much the same as that used for the date, though there are a couple of wrinkles that need to be ironed out.

Here's the basic routine. It uses the **getHours**(), **getMinutes**(), and **getSeconds**() methods to extract the hour, minutes and seconds values from the date, then combines them into a string with ":" between the parts.

```
<HTML>
<HEAD>
<TITLE>Time - version 1</TITLE>
</HEAD>
<BODY>
<SCRIPT>
d = new Date()
hour = d.getHours()
mins = d.getMinutes()
secs = d.getSeconds()

document.write(hour +":" + mins + ":" + secs)
</SCRIPT>
</BODY>
</HTML>
```

Improving the display

At first sight, you may not see any problem with the display. Here, for example, is what the routine has just given me:

14:56:12

But when I reloaded the page a few moments later, I got this:

15:0:4

Single digit values do not look good! They need a leading '0'. The neatest solution here is to use the conditional operator ? : that we looked at in Chapter 4. The expression:

(mins<10) ? ":0" : ":"

will produce ":0" when the minutes are in single digits, and ":" otherwise. We can use this instead of a plain ":" when creating the output string – though note that the whole expression must be enclosed in brackets. Change the output line to read:

```
document.write(hour + ((mins<10) ? ":0" : ":") + mins +
((secs<10) ? ":0" : ":") + secs)
```

It is not a very readable line, and you must make sure that all the opening and closing brackets are in the right places, but the resulting display is far better:

```
15:05:02
```

When is now?

The other problem with this time display is that it will only be right when the page is first opened. Your clock isn't going! If you want to show the right time all the time, it must be up-dated constantly – and for that we need Timeouts. We will come back to this in Chapter 7.

String methods

In JavaScript, strings are objects, not variables as they are in earlier languages. Much of the time this doesn't make a lot of difference – you can treat them as if they were variables – but the String object has properties and methods which can be applied to any strings in your code. You may find some of them useful.

Strictly speaking, a string should be created with a line like this:

```
myString = new String("This is a string of text")
```

In practice, simply assigning a value will work just as well:

```
myString = "This is a string of text"
```

Any text entered at a prompt, in a Text box or TextArea is also a string.

There are two dozen String methods. Many of them simply allow you to do the same kind of formatting in JavaScript as you can in HTML. For example, take the **bold**() method. This emboldens text, in exactly the same way as a <B> tag.

In this example, the lines in the <SCRIPT> and in the main body all produce the same effect:

```
<HTML>
<BODY>
<SCRIPT>
myString = new String("This is a JavaScript string")
document.write("<P>" + myString.bold())
document.write("<P><B>" + myString + "</B>")
</SCRIPT>
<P><B>This is an HTML string</B>
</BODY>
</HTML>
```

These are all listed in the String methods on page 160. It is useful to know that they exist, as sometimes it may be simpler to use a method than a tag. For the rest of this chapter, however, I intend to concentrate on those methods which allow us to do something new with strings.

String slicing

There are several methods that allow you to analyse, divide or otherwise manipulate a string.

charAt(*placeNumber*) returns the character at *placeNumber*, and in strings, as in arrays, you start counting from 0. Try this – it also shows the use of the **length** property.

```
<HTML>
<BODY>
<SCRIPT>
myString = new String("The cat sat on the mat")
len = myString.length
for (n = 0; n < len; n++)
{
    c =  myString.charAt(n)
    document.write("Character "+ n + " is " + c + "<BR>")
}
</SCRIPT>
</BODY>
</HTML>
```

indexOf(*text*) gives you another way of analysing a string. It gives you the first position at which it finds *text* within the string, and *text* may be a character, word or phrase. If *text* is not present, the method retuns -1.

```
if (eMailAddress.indexOf("@") == -1)
    document.write("Invalid e-mail address")
```

lastIndexOf(*text*) does the same as **indexOf()**, but starts from the end of the string and picks up the last occurrence of *text*.

Here are the two in use:

```
<HTML>
<BODY>
<SCRIPT>
myString = new String("The cat sat on the mat")
place = myString.indexOf("cat")
document.write("cat starts at character " + place )
document.write("<P>")
lastplace = myString.lastIndexOf("at")
document.write("The last at starts at character " +lastplace)
</SCRIPT>
</BODY>
</HTML>
```

split(*separator*) chops a string into an array of smaller strings, splitting it where it finds a separator character. You could use it for picking the individual fields out of CSV (comma separated values) data, or for splitting a sentence into words. the method is used in lines like this:

```
wordArray = myString.split(" ")
```

This splits *myString* at the spaces, copying the parts into *wordArray*. Here's a worked example. The string is split using the space as the separator, and a count is kept of the number of spaces. This count is then used to loop through the new array, writing its elements to the screen:

```
<HTML>
<BODY>
<SCRIPT>
myString = new String("The cat sat on the mat")
len = myString.length
```

```
spaces = 0
for (n = 0 ; n < len; n++)
   if (myString.charAt(n) == " ")
      spaces += 1
words = myString.split(" ")
for (n= 0; n <= spaces; n++)
   document.write(words[n] + "<BR>")
</SCRIPT>
</BODY>
</HTML>
```

substring(*start, end*) or **substr(*start, end*)** – the two are all but identical – copies from a string the set of characters from *start* to the one before *end*, counting the first character as 0.

```
myString = new String("The cat sat on the mat")
newString = myString.substring(4,10)
```

This would make *newString* hold "cat sat".

slice(*start, end*) is a variation of **substring()**. Here the size of the new string is determined by end – the position of the last character to be copied.

```
myString = new String("The cat sat on the mat")
newString = myString.slice(4,10)
```

This makes *newString* hold "cat sat on".

Joining strings

str1.**concat**(*str2, str3, ...*) adds the series of *str*ings – variables or literal text – to the base string *str1* to make a new one.

```
surname = "Bloggs"
firstname = "Jo"
title = "Mr"
username = title.concat(" ",firstname, " ", surname)
```

Remember that you can also join strings with the '+' sign. You can 'add' text and strings to make new strings in exactly the same way as you can add them in **write()** expressions. For example, if *visitorName* held "Jo", after this line:

```
greeting = "Hello " + visitorName
```

greeting would hold "Hello Jo".

Slice and join

Here's a final example of the string slicing methods at work. This uses **substring**() alongside the **indexOf** methods to slice the title and surname out of a full name.

```
<HTML>
<BODY>
<SCRIPT>
fullName = prompt("Please enter title and name, e.g. Mr
John Smith","")
firstSpace =  fullName.indexOf(" ")
title = fullName.substring(0,firstSpace)
len = fullName.length
lastSpace = fullName.lastIndexOf(" ")
surname = fullName.substring(lastSpace,len)
user = title + " " + surname
document.write("Hello " + user)
</SCRIPT>
</BODY>
</HTML>
```

Case

There are two methods for changing the case of text.

toLowerCase() converts any capitals in a string to lower case

toUpperCase() converts any lower case to upper case.

Use one or other when comparing strings if you want the comparison to ignore case. Try this simple search routine:

```
<HTML>
<BODY>
<SCRIPT>
baseString = "Be where you want to be with TEACH
YOURSELF"
document.write(baseString + "<BR>")
search = prompt("Enter text to find","")
lowerbase = baseString.toLowerCase()
lowersearch = search.toLowerCase()
foundAt =  lowerbase.indexOf(lowersearch)
if (foundAt > -1)
```

```
        document.write("There was a match at character " +
foundAt)
</SCRIPT>
</BODY>
</HTML>
```

Search and replace

There are three String methods, **match()**, **search()** and **replace()** that work on text using *regular expressions*. These are composed of literal characters, wildcards and special characters that can be used to find inexact matches or to locate text in particular places within strings. They could prove useful in server-side JavaScript when searching databases held on a server. As (a) I cannot conceive of any realistic use for them in client-side JavaScript and (b) they are fiddly and complex, I am not covering them here. You will find a brief summary of these methods on page 161. And if you do find a possible use for them and want to know more, look them up in the Core JavaScript Reference.

Exercises

1 Extend the *cube()* function on page 79 so that it can raise a number to any (integer) power.

2 Write a function *dice()* which generates a random number in the range 1 to 6.

3 A palindrome is a phrase which reads the same backwards as it does forwards, e.g. "rats live on no evil star". Write a function that will test a phrase and return true if it is a palindrome. Some people ignore spaces and punctuation, e.g. 'madam, I'm adam'. This allows more phrases to count as palindromes, but requires more programming.

Summary

• A function is a self-contained block of code, identified by a name.

• Data can be passed to functions through parameters, and passed back through return values.

- A recursive function is one which calls itself – it must have an escape route!

- JavaScript has a set of Math methods that handle random numbers, integers, trigonometry and other key mathematical functions.

- The Date methods allow you to get or set the date or time.

- The String methods give you a range of ways to analyse and manipulate text.

06

forms

In this chapter you will learn

- about form elements
- how to read and validate input data
- how to create single and multiple selection lists
- how to use forms for feedback and interactively

The basic form

Forms are the interactive part of HTML, and the link between you, your readers and your JavaScript code. They are so important to JavaScript that it is worth spending a little time on the relevant HTML tags.

The form itself is not much more than a container, but it can contain buttons, that can be used for controlling code, and text areas and other elements where your reader can enter data or make choices. If you want to give instant feedback to your reader, the simplest way to do it is through an element on a form. If you want your reader to contact you, again, a form offers the simplest solution.

The start and end of the form are marked by the tags **<FORM>** and **</FORM>**. The form can be given a NAME – and this is essential if there is more than one form on the page.

```
<FORM NAME = dataentry>
```

If you want the form data to be sent to you for processing, you must specify how and where through the two keywords METHOD and ACTION. These can each take several options, of which the simplest is:

```
<FORM METHOD = Post ACTION = mailto:your_address>
```

With these settings, the data entered into the form is e-mailed to you when the form is submitted. Some older browsers cannot handle the **mailto** option. If you want feedback from all your readers, you need to use a CGI script (and you will need to talk to your ISP about this).

Buttons and text inputs

Data is collected mainly in <INPUT ...> tags. These come in several vareties, and their nature is defined by the **TYPE** =... option.

<INPUT TYPE = text creates a single line slot for text entry. Text INPUTs need a second option **NAME** =... to identify the variable where the data will be stored.

```
<INPUT TYPE = text NAME = email>
```

This creates the variable *email*. It will be displayed on screen as a blank data entry slot, 20 characters wide. For a different size slot, add the option SIZE = giving the number of characters.

Put some text nearby, so your visitors know what it is for:

```
E-mail address: <INPUT NAME = email SIZE = 30>
```

<INPUT TYPE = button creates a clickable button. The simplest way to run a JavaScript program is from one of these.

```
<INPUT TYPE = button VALUE = "Done" onClick = ...>
```

The **VALUE= "Done"** option defines the label for the button. onClick is followed by the JavaScript code.

If the form data is to be e-mailed on to you, somewhere in it you will a **Submit** button.

```
<INPUT TYPE = Submit VALUE = "Send Now">
```

The phrase:

```
TYPE = Submit
```

defines it as a button that submits feedback. The similar phrase:

```
TYPE = Reset
```

defines a button to clear the form's contents.

```
VALUE = "Send Now"
```

defines the button's caption. You can use any text you like, but you must enclose it in quotes or only the first word will be displayed.

If you want to collect some text that runs over several lines, such as a snail mail address, use a **<TEXTAREA...>** tag.

```
<TEXTAREA NAME = Address>
```

This displays as a very small box with scroll bars to the right and bottom. You can make it into a decent size by adding the options **ROWS** and **COLS** to define the size of the display.

```
<TEXTAREA NAME = Address ROWS = 4 COLS = 40>
```

The ROWS and COLS settings only affect the display size. If your visitors want to write more lines, or longer ones, they can – that's what the scroll bars are there for.

Note that <TEXTAREA> needs a closing </TEXTAREA> tag.

Checkboxes and radios

If you want your form-fillers to be able to choose from a set of alternatives, you should use the TYPE options:

☑ Checkbox where several alternatives can be chosen, or

◉ Radio, where only one of the set can be selected.

They are used in very similar ways, with one significant exception. With checkboxes, each INPUT should have its own NAME variable, to store the response.

```
I am interested in: <BR>
<INPUT TYPE = Checkbox NAME = hard> Hardware <BR>
<INPUT TYPE = Checkbox NAME = soft> Software <BR>
<INPUT TYPE = Checkbox NAME = books> Books <P>
```

If the visitor selects the *Hardware* checkbox, the variable *hard* will have the value *on*.

With radio buttons, the same NAME should be used for all the radios in the set, as you only want to allow one of the alternatives to be chosen:

```
Sex: <BR>
<INPUT TYPE = Radio NAME = sex VALUE = m
CHECKED> Male <BR>
<INPUT TYPE = Radio NAME = sex VALUE = f > Female
```

We now need to add the VALUE = clause. This sets the value to be returned, so that the feedback will be in the form of *sex = dk* (if you have an indecisive visitor). If you omit the VALUE =, the feedback would read *sex = on*, whatever was selected.

Notice the keyword CHECKED in the first <INPUT...> above. This sets the default. Miss it out if you want to start with all the radios clear.

Compare this HTML code with the following screen display.

```
<HTML>
<HEAD>
<TITLE>Checkboxes and Radios</TITLE>
</HEAD>
<BODY>
<FORM METHOD=Post ACTION=mailto://sales@clogs.com>
Tell me more about these wonderful Witherspoon clogs <P>
```

```
Style: <BR>
<INPUT TYPE = Checkbox NAME = trad>Traditional <BR>
<INPUT TYPE = Checkbox NAME = slipon>Slip-on<BR>
<INPUT TYPE = Checkbox NAME = gold>Gold Lame <P>
Sex: <BR>
<INPUT TYPE = Radio NAME = sex> Gents<BR>
<INPUT TYPE = Radio NAME = sex CHECKED> Ladies
 <P> <INPUT TYPE = Submit VALUE = "Send">
<INPUT TYPE = Reset VALUE = "Clear and Restart">
</FORM>
</BODY>
</HTML>
```

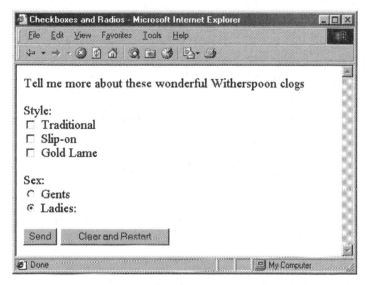

Figure 6.1 This form also has a TYPE = Reset button to clear the form, in case the visitor wants to start again.

Drop-down lists

Drop-down lists are one of the neatest ways of offering a set of alternatives. In HTML they can be implemented with the tags <SELECT ...> and <OPTION = ...>

<SELECT ...> provides the framework for the list. It takes the keyword NAME to define the variable where the selection will be recorded. The matching tag </SELECT> closes the list.

<OPTION = ...> defines an entry for the list. It must have a word in the tag – this will be fed back to you in the SELECT NAME variable – and a label to go on the list. You need an <OPTION = ...> tag for every item.

The tags fit together like this:

```
<SELECT NAME = Level>
   <OPTION = stand> Standard
   <OPTION = prof> Professional
</SELECT>
```

That gives us a drop-down list with two items.

If the visitor selects *Standard*, the *stand* option will be passed to *Level*, and the feedback mail will include this phrase:

```
Level = stand
```

An <OPTION = ...> tag can include the word SELECTED, to set that item as the default.

Look for the line:

```
<OPTION = Win SELECTED> PC/Windows
```

in this next example, and notice how the item *PC/Windows* is displayed at the top of the list, in the selection slot – though its natural place is further down.

```
<HTML>
<HEAD>
<TITLE>Drop-down Lists</TITLE>
</HEAD>
<BODY>
<H2> Order Form </H2>
<FORM METHOD=Post ACTION=mailto:sales@pcs.co.uk>
Order your software here: <P>
Platform: <SELECT NAME = Platform>
   <OPTION = Pcdos > PC/DOS
   <OPTION = Mac> Mac
   <OPTION = Unix> Unix
   <OPTION = Win SELECTED> PC/Windows
</SELECT>
```

```
Level: <SELECT NAME = Level>
   <OPTION = stand> Standard
   <OPTION = prof> Professional
</SELECT> <P>
<INPUT TYPE = Submit VALUE = "Send" >
</FORM>
</BODY>
</HTML>
```

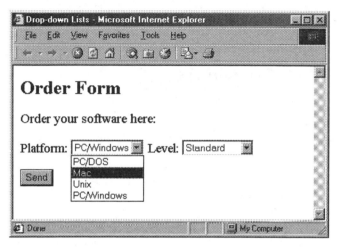

Figure 6.2 Drop-down lists are good for multiple choices.

Buttons

The **<BUTTON>** tag is a flexible alternative to **<INPUT TYPE = Reset/Submit>** for creating clickable buttons. If all you want is a standard 'Submit', then it takes a little more work to do it this way, with no advantage. Compare these two lines. They produce identical results:

```
<BUTTON TYPE="submit"> Send me </BUTTON>
<INPUT TYPE = "submit" VALUE = "Send me">
```

A **<BUTTON>** tag gives you more control over what appears on the button. You can format the text:

```
<BUTTON TYPE="submit"><FONT SIZE = 5 COLOR = red>
<B> Send me </B></FONT></BUTTON>
```

This gives you large, bold, red characters on the button.

You can even use an image instead of text…

```
<BUTTON TYPE="submit"> <IMG SRC = "sendme.gif"> </
BUTTON>
```

…or as well as text:

```
<BUTTON TYPE ="submit"> <FONT SIZE = 6> Send me
please</FONT> <img src = "smiley.gif"></BUTTON>
```

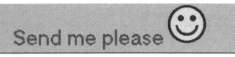

Submit image buttons

There is a special <INPUT TYPE = …> option that is worth knowing about.

```
<INPUT TYPE = "image" SRC = "sendme.gif">
```

This displays the image, but makes it work as a submit button. The advantage of this is that it does not have the standard grey, rectangular background, which you get with <BUTTON>, but it can only be used for submitting forms.

The elements array

The text boxes, options, buttons and other elements that you place on a form are automatically made into an array. When each element is a totally separate item, and is treated individually, this array is irrelevant, but at other times it can be very useful. If you need to access or change the values in a set of items, for example, treating them as an array can be the simplest way to do it.

The array is always called *elements[]*. The elements are numbered in the order in which they appear on the form, starting in the top left with *elements[0]*.

In this example, an array-based routine is used to clear the entries from some of the text boxes on a form. This allows visitors to erase the choices they have made, without also clearing their name and e-mail address. Compare this with the effect of the Reset button, which would wipe all the boxes clear.

Note that the loop runs from 2 to 4, picking up the 'Order...' text boxes only. After you have got this working, change the end value to read 'loop < 7' and see what happens when you let it run onto the buttons.

```
<HTML>
<HEAD>
<TITLE>Arrays of elements</TITLE>
<SCRIPT>
function clearform()
{
    for(loop = 2; loop < 5; loop++)
        document.form1.elements[loop].value = ""
}
</SCRIPT>
</HEAD>
<BODY>
<H2>Order form</H2>
<FORM NAME = form1>
Contact name <INPUT TYPE = text NAME = username
VALUE = ""> <BR>
E-mail addess <INPUT TYPE = text NAME = email  VALUE
= ""> <BR>
```

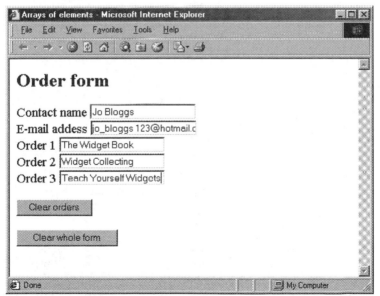

Figure 6.3 Clear orders just wipes the Order... text boxes

```
Order 1 <INPUT TYPE = text NAME = order1 VALUE = "" >
<BR>
Order 2 <INPUT TYPE = text NAME = order2 VALUE = "" >
<BR>
Order 3 <INPUT TYPE = text NAME = order3 VALUE = "" >
<BR>
<P><INPUT TYPE = button VALUE = "Clear orders" onClick
= "clearform()">
<P><INPUT TYPE = Reset VALUE = "Clear whole form">
</FORM>
</BODY>
```

Checking entries

If a form is to be completed properly, some items of data may be essential – you must have the visitor's address if you are to send them something. Other entries may have to fall into a certain range of values – dates and order numbers must be valid.

Is there anything there?

You can easily check whether or not data has been entered into a text box, and with relatively little code, you can send your visitor back to enter something. Attach this to any text box or text area if you don't want your visitors to leave it blank:

```
onBlur = "if(this.value=='') {alert('Data please');this.focus()}"
```

this refers to whichever object it is attached to. If it is empty (value== ''), the following commands, held in {curly brackets}, will be executed.

The **focus()** method places the cursor in a text box. (It also activates pages, highlights buttons and selects other objects.)

this.focus() puts the cursor into the current box. It works reliably when run from code within the event handler, though can get confused if used in code in functions. Somewhere in the process of transferring from page to function it can lose track of which element **this** refers to.

I like to keep event handling code as simple as possible, so in the next example, this kind of checking is managed by the function *checkData()*. The *elements[]* array number of the text box is passed to it, e.g.

```
    onBlur = checkData(2)
```

The function then checks and responds as above.

```
function checkData(box)
{
    if(document.form1.elements[box].value == "")
    {
        alert("Please complete this box")
        document.form1.elements[box].focus()
    }
}
```

If you have several essential text boxes, this is a neater solution than attaching code directly to each.

Is it right?

Validation is another matter. Some things can be checked without too much trouble.

Is a number value in the right range?

```
checknum = eval(document.form.element[n].value)
if (checknum < 0 || checknum > 999)
    error routine...
```

Does the text box contain (unwanted) digits?

```
digits = false
text = document.form.elements[n].value
for (loop = 0; loop < text.length; loop++)
    {
    c = text.value.charAt(loop)
    if (c >= "0" && c <= "9")
        digits = true
    }
    if (digits)
        error routine...
```

The *validate( )* function in the example checks an ISBN (book number). If you were doing this by hand, you would take each digit in turn, multiply the first by 1, the second by 2, and so on up to the last but one. The results are then added together and the total divided by 11. The remainder should be the same as the last digit.

For example, the ISBN of this book is 0 340 81129 3. Do the sum:

$1*0 + 2*3 + 3*4 + 4*0 + 5*8 + 6*1 + 7*1 + 8*2 + 9*9 = 168/11$
$= 15$ remainder 3

The routine works through the ISBN, copying the numbers into an array, and ignoring spaces. If there aren't 10 digits, the code stops there and reports the error. The total is calculated and the modulus operator (%) used to find the remainder.

The notes on the program should help you to follow it in detail – but if you prefer, you could substitute a simple number range check instead and forget ISBNs!

```html
<HTML>
<HEAD>
<TITLE>Validate</TITLE>
<SCRIPT>
function checkData(box)
{
    if(document.form1.elements[box].value == "")
    {
        alert("Please complete this box")
        document.form1.elements[box].focus()
    }
}

function validate()
{
    num = new Array(10)
    count = 0
    total = 0
    number = document.form1.isbn.value
    for(loop = 0; loop < number.length; loop++)
    {
        digit = number.charAt(loop)
        if(digit >= "0" && digit <= 9)
        {
            num[count] = eval(digit)
            count++
        }
        if (count == 10) break
    }
```

```
    if (count < 10)
        return false
    for(loop = 0; loop < 9; loop++)
    {
        total += num[loop] * (loop +1)
    }
    if((total % 11) == num[9])
        return true
    else return false
}
</SCRIPT>
</HEAD>
<BODY>
<H1 ALIGN=CENTER>Buk-U-Like</H1>
<H2 ALIGN=CENTER>On-line Order Form</H2>
<FORM NAME = form1 METHOD = post ACTION =
mailto:sales@bukulike.co.uk>
<P>Your e-mail address:
<INPUT TYPE = text NAME = email SIZE = 30 onBlur =
"checkData(0)">
<P>Name:
<INPUT TYPE = text NAME = buyer SIZE = 30 >
<P>Title of book:
<INPUT TYPE = text NAME = title SIZE = 40 onBlur =
"checkData(2)">
<P>ISBN (essential)
<INPUT TYPE = text NAME = isbn SIZE = 15 onBlur =
"if(validate()==false) {alert('Invalid ISBN');this.focus}">
<P><INPUT TYPE = Submit VALUE = Send>
</FORM>
<SCRIPT>
document.form1.email.focus()
</SCRIPT>
</BODY>
</HTML>
```

Reading checkboxes and radios

Checkboxes and radios are handled in very similar ways. The main difference is how they are identified from within JavaScript. If we take the examples on page 103:

```
<INPUT TYPE = Checkbox NAME = trad>Traditional <BR>
```

```
...
<INPUT TYPE = Radio NAME = sex> Gents<BR>
<INPUT TYPE = Radio NAME = sex CHECKED> Ladies
```

◆ Checkboxes can be recognized, as normal, by NAME:

```
document.form1.trad
```

◆ Radio buttons, having only one NAME per set, are formed into arrays, numbered in order of their appearance:

```
document.form1.sex[0]
```

Checkboxes and Radio buttons have a **checked** property, which is *true* when they are selected. We can test the *resources* Checkbox with:

```
if (document.form1.trad.checked == true)
```

The test works just as well if you omit **==true**

```
if (document.form1.trad.checked)
```

The same approach works for Radio buttons:

```
if (document.form1.sex[0].checked)
```

If you are going to check an option more than once, or in complex expressions, you will get neater and more readable code by linking the option to a variable. This can be set by the **onClick** event handler.

You cannot simply do this:

```
<INPUT TYPE = Checkbox NAME = trad onClick = "tradVar
= true">
```

The problem is that checkboxes and radio buttons are *toggles* – clicking them switches their state between *on* or *off*. You must test the **checked** property.

```
onClick = "tradVar = (this.checked ? true : false)"
```

this refers to the current object – the checkbox. **this.checked** will return true if the checkbox is selected, and the ? : conditional test will set *tradVar* to true or false accordingly.

You can simplify the expression by just copying the value of **checked** into the variable:

```
onClick = "tradVar = this.checked"
```

The next example shows these approaches in use. Notice that the **Submit** button has been replaced by one labelled 'Action', which calls up the *process()* function. If you want the feedback e-mailed to you, it is simpler to stick to standard HTML. Use JavaScript when you want to find out information so that you can respond to your visitors while they are on-line. Here, all that happens is that alert boxes show the settings. In practice, you might use the selections to determine which page to display next, or what to write on that page.

```
<HTML>
<HEAD>
<SCRIPT>
function process()
{
if (searcheng == true)
    alert("Search selected")
if (software)
    alert("Software sites selected")
if (document.form1.resources.checked)
    alert("JavaScript resources selected")
if (document.form1.mlist[0].checked)
    alert("Include on mailing list")
else
    alert("Leave off the list")
}
</SCRIPT>
</HEAD>
<BODY>
<SCRIPT>
searcheng = false
software = false
</SCRIPT>
<FORM NAME = form1>
Which types of links would you like
<P>Style:
<BR><INPUT TYPE = Checkbox NAME = search onClick =
"searcheng = this.checked"> Search engines
<BR><INPUT TYPE = Checkbox NAME = softsites onClick =
"software = ((this.checked)?true:false)"> Software sites
<BR><INPUT TYPE = Checkbox NAME = resources>
JavaScript resources
```

```
<P> Join our mailing list?
<BR><INPUT TYPE = Radio NAME = mlist> Yes please
<BR><INPUT TYPE = Radio NAME = mlist CHECKED> No
thanks
<P><INPUT TYPE = Submit VALUE = "Action" onClick =
"process()">
</FORM>
</BODY>
</HTML>
```

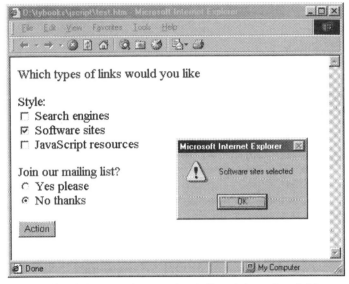

Figure 6.4 Using an alert to check the status of variables.

Single selection lists

Drop-down lists created by the <SELECT> and <OPTION> tags have two forms. One allows only one selection at a time; the other accepts multiple selections. They need to be handled in different ways.

A <SELECT> list has a **selectedIndex** property which is the key to reading the list. If you have set up a list in *form1* with:

```
<SELECT NAME = choice>
```

then this will give you the index:

```
chosen = document.form1.choice.selectedIndex
```

You can then use the index value in a set of **if** tests, to react to the selection, or – as in the example – use it to pick out an element from an array. Here, the array holds prices and the function *setPrice()* displays the price of the selected item.

```
function setPrice()
{
    chosen =document.form1.choice.selectedIndex
    document.form1.price.value = prices[chosen]
}
```

Here's the code. Feel free to substitute your own data!

```
<HTML>
<HEAD>
<TITLE>Single selections</TITLE>
<SCRIPT>
prices = new Array(5)
    prices[0] =19.99
    prices[1] = 24.99
    prices[2] =29.99
    prices[3] =39.49
    prices[4] =9.95
function setPrice()
{
    chosen =document.form1.choice.selectedIndex
    document.form1.price.value = prices[chosen]
}
</SCRIPT>
</HEAD>


<BODY>
<H3>Witherspoon clogs</H3>
<FORM NAME = form1>
Style <SELECT NAME = choice>
<OPTION = trad>Traditional
<OPTION = slipon>Slip on
<OPTION = cloth>Fine worsted
<OPTION = gold>Gold lame
<OPTION = kids>Child
</SELECT>
<P> <P> <P>
Price: <INPUT TYPE = text NAME = price VALUE = "">
<P>
```

```
<INPUT TYPE = button VALUE = "Show price" onClick =
"setPrice()">
</FORM>
</BODY>
</HTML>
```

Figure 6.5 Using an alert to check the status of variables.

Multiple selections

If you write the **MULTIPLE** keyword into a <**SELECT**> tag, your visitors will be able to select more than one option (in the usual way – by holding down [Control] while clicking).

```
<SELECT MULTIPLE NAME = os>
```

The **selectIndex** of the whole <**SELECT**> set is then no longer of use. We now need to use the **selected** property (a *true* or *false* value) of the individual <**OPTION**>s. These form an array, the name of which comes from the <**SELECT**> tag, and can be conveniently tested in a loop:

```
for(loop = 0; loop <document.form1.os.length; loop++)
    if (document.form1.os[loop].selected)
```

♦ **document.form1.os.length** tells you the number of <OPTION>s in the set.

♦ **document.form1.os[loop].selected** returns the state of the <OPTION> identified by the index – it is *true* if selected.

<OPTION>s have a **text** property which is the text displayed in the drop-down list. You might want to include this in feedback to yourself, or to display it on screen so that your visitors can confirm their selections.

In the next example, visitors are asked to select the IT courses that interest them. When they click the 'Show selection' button, the *show()* function will check through the array and add the text of selected options to the *temp* string, then copy the finished string into the TEXTAREA for display.

```
<HTML>
<HEAD>
<TITLE>Multiple Selections</TITLE>
<SCRIPT>
function show()
{
    temp = ""
    for(loop = 0; loop < document.form1.it.length; loop++)
        if (document.form1.it[loop].selected)
            temp = temp + document.form1.it[loop].text + " "
    document.form1.showit.value = temp
}
</SCRIPT>
</HEAD>
<BODY>
<H3>Tel me more about courses on ...</H3>
<FORM NAME = form1>
<SELECT MULTIPLE NAME = it>
<OPTION = windows>Windows
<OPTION = word>Word
<OPTION = excel>Excel
<OPTION = access>Access
<OPTION = web>World Wide Web
<OPTION = email>E-mail
</SELECT>
<INPUT TYPE = button VALUE = "Show selection" onClick =
"show()">
<P><TEXTAREA NAME = showit ROWS = 2 COLS = 40>
</TEXTAREA>
</FORM>
</BODY>
</HTML>
```

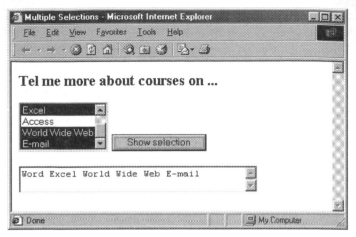

Figure 6.6 Use the MULTIPLE setting when several options can be selected.

Feedback on-line

The next example pulls together some aspects of using FORM options in JavaScript, gives immediate feedback to the user and also generates e-mail feedback to the page's author.

At Wheeler Dealers you can insure your cycle on-line. The cost of the insurance is based on the value of the cycle, but varies with the region and with the level of cover. This information is entered into or selected from options in the form: *region* is a drop-down list; *cover* is a set of Radio buttons. Both could have been done either way, as in both cases only one item is being selected from a set.

The basic formula is:

£10 + (value of cycle/100) * regional rate * cover level

The premium is worked out in the function *calculate()*. Here are the crucial lines:

```
howmuch = eval(document.form1.InsVal.value)
```

eval() is necessary to convert the text into a numeric value.

```
for(loop = 0; loop < document.form1.cover.length; loop++)
    if (document.form1.cover[loop].checked)
```

Radio button sets do not have a **selectedIndex** property. To find out which one was selected, we have to test the **checked** property of each button in the array.

```
level = loop + 1
```

This gives cover levels of 1, 2 or 3 – a crude multiplier. If you were doing this properly, you would probably want to select the level from an array of values. This has been done with the regional rates.

```
where = document.form1.region.selectedIndex
cost = eval(10 + howmuch / 100 * rate[where] * level)
document.form1.quote.value = cost
```

Note the 'Purchase' button. This calls up the *confirmPurchase()* function which runs a confirm dialog box before sending the e-mail with the command:

```
document.form1.submit()
```

submit( ) is equivalent to the tag **<INPUT TYPE = Submit>**.

```
<HTML>
<HEAD>
<TITLE>Feedback</TITLE>
<SCRIPT>
rate = new Array(4)
rate[0] = 10
rate[1] = 8
rate[2] = 6
rate[3] = 7
rate[4] = 12
function calculate() {
    howmuch = eval(document.form1.InsVal.value)
    for(loop = 0; loop < document.form1.cover.length; loop++)
        if (document.form1.cover[loop].checked)
            level = loop + 1
    where =document.form1.region.selectedIndex
    cost = eval(10 + howmuch / 100 * rate[where] * level)
    document.form1.quote.value = cost
}

function confirmPurchase() {
    if (confirm("I want to take up this offer"))
        document.form1.submit()
}
```

```
</SCRIPT>
</HEAD>
<BODY>
<H1 ALIGN=CENTER>Wheeler Dealers</H1>
<FORM NAME = form1 METHOD = post ACTION =
"mailto:sales@wdeals.co.uk">
<P><B>Value of cycle:</B>
<INPUT TYPE = text NAME = InsVal SIZE = 10>
<P>Region
<SELECT NAME = region>
<OPTION = london>London
<OPTION = southeast>South East
<OPTION = southwest>South West
<OPTION = rest>Rest of England
<OPTION = wales>Wales
</SELECT>
<P>Type of cover
<BR><INPUT TYPE = Radio NAME = cover>Third Party
<BR><INPUT TYPE = Radio NAME = cover>Third Party Fire
```

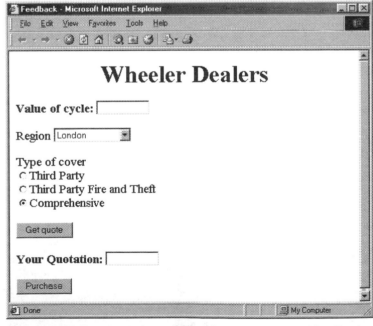

Figure 6.7 Forms can be used for data collection and feedback.

```
and Theft
<BR><INPUT TYPE = Radio NAME = cover
CHECKED>Comprehensive
<P><INPUT TYPE = "button" NAME = "calc" VALUE = "Get
quote" onClick = "calculate()">
<P><B>Your Quotation:<B>
<INPUT TYPE = text NAME = quote SIZE = 10>
<P><INPUT TYPE = button NAME = done VALUE = Pur-
chase onClick = "confirmPurchase()">
</FORM>
</BODY>
</HTML>
```

Keep this example safe as you will need it in Chapter 8.

A JavaScript calculator

In the last example in this chapter, a form is used to create a calculator. Numbers are entered and operations selected by clicking buttons, and the results are displayed in a text box.

The code is rather long, but can be produced in less time than you might think. Cut, paste and edit is the trick! The lines that create the buttons are all virtually the same, and there are some very similar lines in the *doFunc()* and *calculate()* functions.

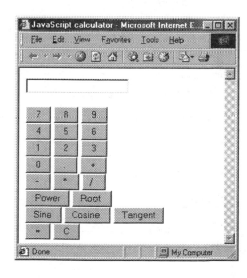

Figure 6.8 Here the form simply acts as a container for the buttons and text box.

Here is what happens when the buttons are clicked:

- Numbers and decimal point – pass the button value to *doNum()* to add the display box.

- Operators – pass the operator to *doOp()* which stores in *n1* the current value in the display box and stores the operator in op. It then clears the box for the next number.

- Equals sign – runs *calculate()* which takes *n1* and the current value in the display and combines them according to the current value of *op*.

- Root, Sine, Cosine and Tangent – these call *doFunc()* which uses the Math methods to work out the values. Note how it converts angle values from degrees to radians using *toRad()*.

```
<HTML>
<HEAD>
<TITLE>JavaScript calculator</TITLE>
<SCRIPT>
function doNum(x)
{
    f1.display.value = f1.display.value + x
}
function doOp(operation) {
    n1 = eval(f1.display.value)
    op = operation
    f1.display.value = ""
}
function toRad(deg) {
    return deg / 360 * 2 * Math.PI
}
function doFunc(fn) {
    n1 = eval(f1.display.value)
    angle = toRad(n1)
    if (fn == "r")
        f1.display.value = Math.sqrt(n1)
    else if (fn == "s")
        f1.display.value = Math.sin(angle)
    else if (fn == "c")
        f1.display.value = Math.cos(angle)
    else if (fn == "t")
        f1.display.value = Math.tan(angle)
}
```

```
function calculate() {
    n2 = eval(f1.display.value)
    if (op == "+")
        f1.display.value = n1 + n2
    else if (op == "-")
        f1.display.value = n1 - n2
    else if (op == "*")
        f1.display.value = n1 * n2
    else if (op == "/")
        f1.display.value = n1 / n2
    else if (op == "p")
        f1.display.value = Math.pow(n1, n2)
}
function doClear() {
    f1.display.value = ""
}
</SCRIPT>
</HEAD>
<BODY>
<SCRIPT>
var n1 = 0
var op = "+"
var n2 = 0
</SCRIPT>
<FORM NAME = f1>
<INPUT TYPE = text NAME = display>
<P>
<INPUT TYPE = button VALUE = " 7 " onClick = doNum("7")>
<INPUT TYPE = button VALUE = " 8 " onClick = doNum("8")>
<INPUT TYPE = button VALUE = " 9 " onClick = doNum("9")>
<BR>
<INPUT TYPE = button VALUE = " 4 " onClick = doNum("4")>
<INPUT TYPE = button VALUE = " 5 " onClick = doNum("5")>
<INPUT TYPE = button VALUE = " 6 " onClick = doNum("6")>
<BR>
<INPUT TYPE = button VALUE = " 1 " onClick = doNum("1")>
<INPUT TYPE = button VALUE = " 2 " onClick = doNum("2")>
<INPUT TYPE = button VALUE = " 3 " onClick = doNum("3")>
<BR>
<INPUT TYPE = button VALUE = " 0 " onClick = doNum("0")>
<INPUT TYPE = button VALUE = " . " onClick = doNum(".")>
<INPUT TYPE = button VALUE = " + " onClick =doOp("+")>
<BR>
```

```
<INPUT TYPE = button VALUE = "  -   " onClick = doOp("-")>
<INPUT TYPE = button VALUE = "  *   " onClick = doOp("*")>
<INPUT TYPE = button VALUE = "  /   " onClick = doOp("/")>
<BR>
<INPUT TYPE = button VALUE = " Power " onClick =
doOp("p")>
<INPUT TYPE = button VALUE = " Root  " onClick =
doFunc("r")> <BR>
<INPUT TYPE = button VALUE = " Sine  " onClick =
doFunc("s")>
<INPUT TYPE = button VALUE = "Cosine " onClick =
doFunc("c")>
<INPUT TYPE = button VALUE = "Tangent" onClick =
doFunc("t")> <BR>
<INPUT TYPE = button VALUE = "  =   " onClick = calculate()>
<INPUT TYPE = button VALUE = "  C   " onClick = doClear()>
</FORM>
</HTML>
```

Exercises

1   Starting from the validate example (page 110), add a field to
collect the price and a function to check that it is within an
acceptable range.

2   Set up a form to collect on-line orders for a business that you
work with, or would like to work in. What data do you need
to collect from customers? How can this be validated? What
calculations will be needed?

3   Set up an array of Web URLs with the matching names in a
SELECT list. Using the **selectedIndex** property of the list as
the index of the array, enable people to select a site from the
list and go to the site. Your code should have a function
something like this, where choice is the SELECT list and
link[] is the array of URLs.

```
function setURL()
{
    where =document.form1.choice.selectedIndex
    window.location = link[where]
}
```

window.location loads the link into the current window.

Summary

- Forms offer a way for your visitors to interact with your code.

- Data can be collected or selected in different types of INPUTs.

- The elements on a form can be identified by name or by their position in the elements array.

- Data should be validated if possible.

- With JavaScript you can give immediate feedback to visitors.

- Forms can also be used as containers for buttons and fields for other interactive programs.

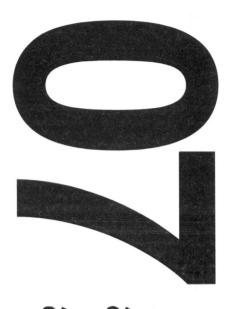

07
animation and images

In this chapter you will learn

- about computer animation
- how to use timeouts for timing
- how to animate text and images
- how to make images clickable

Computer animation

The basis of computer animation is the timed succession of changing images (or text) on screen. For effective animation therefore you need to be able to control timing, the images and the screen display.

Animation in JavaScript is limited by the fact that you only have real control over two of these — the timing and the images. The screen display is largely set when the page is first loaded. You cannot write or draw on the screen in 'real time', nor can you move objects around on it. However, you can change the contents of the Status bar, text boxes and text areas, and you can change the SRC of the image that is displayed in an <IMG > tag. These give us some possibilities that are worth exploiting. But first, you need to know how to control timing.

Timing and timeouts

If you want things to happen after a set period, there are two ways to achieve it. The first, and apparently simplest, uses a loop like this:

```
for (delay = 0; delay < 10000; delay++)
{
    // do nothing
}
```

That just makes the computer twiddle its bits while time passes. Unfortunately, it is virtually useless for animation in JavaScript as JavaScript executes the whole of a function before passing control of the system back to the browser to update the screen.

The second approach uses *timeouts*. A timeout allows you to set a delay before a command is executed. At the simplest, you just give the **setTimeout**() method the job to do and the number of milliseconds to wait before doing it. For example

```
setTimeout("alert('You have been here 5 seconds')",5000)
```

Five seconds after the page has loaded, an alert will pop up. Notice those quotes around the command — they are crucial! If you miss them out, the command will be executed, but the delay will be ignored.

If you want the action repeated at regular intervals, the Timeout must be written into the action, setting it up for the next time.

```
function irritate()
{
    reply = confirm("Enjoying your visit?")
    if (reply == true)
        setTimeout("irritate()",5000)
}
```

Once this has been started, by an *irritate()* somewhere in the main script, it will run every five seconds until the visitor clicks 'Cancel'. This may look like a recursive function (see page 80) but it isn't. The last line does not call the function, but sets up a timeout that will run it again in five seconds.

If you want to be able to stop the repetition, either make the call dependent on a test, as above, or use the **clearTimeout**() method. This needs to know which timeout to clear – there can be any number running at once – so the **setTimeout**() must be created in a slightly different form, giving it a name.

```
timer1 = setTimeout("irritate()", 10000)
...
clearTimeout(timer1)
```

The next example puts a mock visitor counter on the page, updating it constantly – set a suitable delay to reflect your page's popularity!

```
<HTML>
<HEAD>
<TITLE>Timed visits</TITLE>
<SCRIPT>
function addvisitor()
{
    counter++
    document.form1.showcount.value = counter
    delay = Math.random() * 1000 + 1000
    timer = setTimeout("addvisitor()",delay)
}
</SCRIPT>
</HEAD>
```

```
<BODY>
<SCRIPT>
counter = Math.round(Math.random() * 10000) + 1000
</SCRIPT>
<FORM NAME = form1>
Visitors to this page:
<INPUT TYPE = text NAME = showcount VALUE = "">
<P><INPUT TYPE = button VALUE = "I do not believe
you" onClick = "clearTimeout(timer)">
</FORM>
<SCRIPT>
addvisitor()
</SCRIPT>
</BODY>
</HTML>
```

A JavaScript clock

Back on page 91, we looked at the problems of displaying time values neatly. But that only showed the time once. Using timeouts we can now build on this to create a JavaScript clock.

The routine which displays the time is virtually the same as the 'improved' one on page 92, with two differences. The first is that in this script, the time is displayed in a text box, as this can be updated without having to reload the page. The second is that the code has been made into a function called *dotime()*. This allows us to call it with a timeout. Look for this line at the end of the function:

```
clocktime = setTimeout("dotime()",1000)
```

Notice also that the timeout has been assigned to a variable, so that we can turn off the clock with a **clearTimeout(clocktime)**.

```
<HTML>
<HEAD>
<TITLE>Clock</TITLE>
<SCRIPT>
function dotime()
{
    d = new Date()
    h = d.getHours()
```

```
      m = d.getMinutes()
      s = d.getSeconds()
      time = h + ((m<10) ? ":0" : ":") + m + ((s<10) ? ":0" : ":") + s
      document.timeform.time.value = time
      clocktime = setTimeout("dotime()",1000)
}
</SCRIPT>
</HEAD>
<BODY>
<FORM NAME = timeform>
<P>The time is
<INPUT TYPE = text NAME = time VALUE = "" SIZE = 8>
<P><INPUT TYPE = button VALUE = "Stop the clock"
onClick = "clearTimeout(clocktime)">
</FORM>
<SCRIPT>
dotime()
</SCRIPT>
</BODY>
</HTML>
```

Scrolling text

If you have spent any time browsing the Web, you must have
come across scrolling messages in the Status line – many, many
times! Here's how it's done.

To get the text to scroll, we use the **substring**() method to chop
off the first character and move it to the end of the string. This
is best done in four stages.

First find the length of the string:

```
len = phrase.length
```

Now cut it into two parts: *first* holds the first character (0); *rest*
takes the remainder of the string (1 to *len*)

```
first = phrase.substring(0,1)
rest = phrase.substring(1,len)
```

Finally, join the substrings, back to front.

```
phrase = rest + first
```

If you like complicated lines, this will do the same job:

```
phrase = phrase.substring(1,phrase.length) +
phrase.substring(0,1)
```

This code, as it stands, will only scroll one character. If you put it into a loop, it will whistle through so fast that you won't see anything happening. The solution is to use a timeout, so that there is a delay between each repetition of the code. Here, the delay is set to 100 which produces a pause of 1/10th of a second. If your message is shorter, you may find that a longer delay produces a better result.

The *stopscroll()* function is optional. As the whole point of scrolling is to catch the visitors' attention, letting them turn off the scroll is a bit counter-productive – except that they may stay longer on the page once the distraction has been removed!

Notice the use of the variable *phrase*. It is set up and assigned a value in the body SCRIPT, but because a variable created here has global scope, it can be read and altered in the function.

```
<HTML>
<HEAD>
<TITLE>Scroller</TITLE>
<SCRIPT>
function setstatus()
{
    len = phrase.length
    first = phrase.substring(0,1)
    rest = phrase.substring(1,len)
    phrase = rest + first
    self.status = phrase
    timerID = setTimeout("setstatus()",100)
}

function stopscroll()
{
    clearTimeout(timerID)
    self.status = 'Teach Yourself JavaScript'
}
</SCRIPT>
</HEAD>
```

```
<BODY>
<FORM>
<INPUT TYPE = button VALUE = "Stop that scroll!"
onClick = "stopscroll()">
</FORM>
<SCRIPT>
phrase = new String("...Teach Yourself something new
today ... ")
setstatus()
</SCRIPT>
</BODY>
</HTML>
```

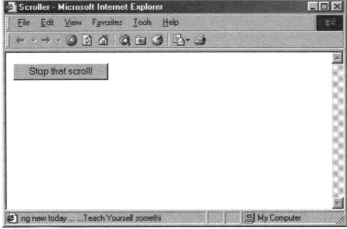

Figure 7.1 A scrolling Status bar will attract attention.

Image objects

Images can be created in two ways – with the <IMG> tag and
with the **Image**() constructor.

<IMG> images

<IMG> images are, of course, placed on the form and have a
whole set of properties, including *height*, *width*, *hspace* and
vspace that can be used to format their position, size and appearance. JavaScript can set these, but cannot change them once
the page has been loaded. The SCR, however, can be changed.

The images are automatically formed into the array *images[]*, and numbered in the order of their position in the document. So the first image can be referred to as *document.images[0]*.

<IMG> images have three event handlers: **onLoad** is triggered by successful loading, **onAbort** and **onError** are triggered when loading is cancelled or fails. You will notice that they do not respond to mouse clicks or movements. There is a way round this, as you will see shortly.

Image()

Image() images are a type of variable and are stored in memory. They allow you to preload images for later display and are especially useful in animation and other situations where you want to be able to drop in a new image quickly without the downloading delay.

```
storedImage = new Image()
storedImage.src = "newpic.gif"
```

This sets up the Image() objects, *storedImage* and assigns to it the image *newpic.gif*. Note the *src* property is used here in exactly the same way as SRC in an IMG tag.

```
tinyImage = new Image(50,25)
tinyImage.src = "newpic.gif"
```

These lines set up a second Image() objects, *tinyImage*, but in this the optional width and height parameters were given. Though the same image, newpic.gif, is loaded, it will be held in a reduced form, 50 pixels wide and 25 pixels high.

An **Image()** object has the same properties as an <IMG> plus a couple more. The most important of these is *complete*, which is set to *true* when the image has been fully downloaded.

Image formats

Web browsers – and therefore JavaScript – can only handle graphics files in two formats – GIF and JPEG (with a .JPEG or .JPG extension). If you want to create your own images, you will need a suitable graphics application, such as Paint Shop Pro. With this you can draw new images or convert images from another application into GIF or JPEG format.

If there is a possibility that the file may not have fully down-loaded before your code wants to use the image, you should check that it is there:

```
if (myPic.complete)
    use the image
else do something else while you wait
```

There's one big restriction on the amount of animation that you can do in JavaScript – you cannot change the position of images on the page, once the page has been loaded. However, you can change the picture held in an <IMG>, and that's how you can get your animation. Here is a simple example to show how to change an <IMG> source. You will need two suitable GIFs for this. I've used stick men, but I'm sure that you can do better – change the filenames to match. Things to notice:

• The image files are loaded into Image() objects in a script in the body, so that they are available when the functions need to use them.

• The functions check that the images are complete, and will only attempt to pass them to the <IMG> if they are.

```
<HTML>
<HEAD>
<SCRIPT>
function bend()
{
    if(pic2.complete)
    pagePic.src = pic2.src
}
function stand()
{
    if(pic1.complete)
    pagePic.src = pic1.src
}
</SCRIPT>
</HEAD>
<BODY>
<IMG SRC = "man1.gif" NAME = pagePic>
<FORM>
<INPUT TYPE = button VALUE = "Knees bend" onClick =
"bend()">
```

```
<INPUT TYPE = button
VALUE = "Stand up"
onClick = "stand()">
</FORM>
<SCRIPT>
pic1 = new Image()
pic1.src = "man1.gif"
pic2 = new Image()
pic2.src = "man2.gif"
</SCRIPT>
</BODY>
</HTML>
```

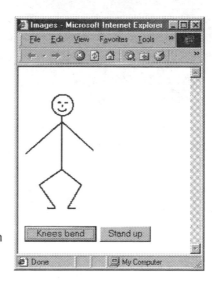

Figure 7.2 If you click the buttons fast enough, you can animate it – there must be a better way! Read on…

Simple animation

Unlike <IMG>s, image() objects are not automatically put into an array, which is a bit of a shame because you often need them in one. If you want to display a sequence of images, the simplest way to do it is to store them in an array, then run the array through a loop.

To set up an array, first load the images into separate objects, then create a new array, giving it the names of the objects. In the example, there are six image files.

```
pic0 = new Image()
pic0.src = "pic0.gif"
pic1 = new Image()
pic1.src = "pic1.gif"
…
pictures = new Array(pic0,pic1,pic2,pic3, pic4, pic5)
```

You now have a simple means to assign a new image. Here's the line at the top of the *animate()* function:

```
pagePic.src = pictures[current++].src
```

This assigns the selected image to the *pagePic* <IMG>. *current* is then incremented ready for next time.

Notice also the line at the end of the function which sets a timeout so that *animate()* is constantly rerun.

```
setTimeout("animate()",200)
```

The *checkload()* function checks the **complete** property of the sixth image, and will not allow the code to reach the *animate()* function until the files are fully loaded. It won't appear to do anything while you are testing the page on your system – as the files will be accessible almost instantly – but it will be useful when the page in online and people view it over the Web.

```
<HTML>
<HEAD>
  <SCRIPT>
  function loadImages()
  {
      pic0 = new Image()
      pic0.src = "pic0.gif"
      pic1 = new Image()
      pic1.src = "pic1.gif"
      pic2 = new Image()
      pic2.src = "pic2.gif"
      pic3 = new Image()
      pic3.src = "pic3.gif"
      pic4 = new Image()
      pic4.src = "pic4.gif"
      pic5 = new Image()
      pic5.src = "pic5.gif"
      pictures = new Array(pic0,pic1,pic2,pic3, pic4, pic5)
  }
  function animate()
  {
      pagePic.src = pictures[current++].src
      if (current == 6)
          current = 0
      setTimeout("animate()",200)
  }
  function checkload()
  {
      if (pic5.complete == false)
          setTimeout("checkload()", 100)
  }
```

```
</SCRIPT>
</HEAD>
<BODY>
<IMG SRC = "pic0.gif" NAME = pagePic>
<SCRIPT>
    current = 1
    loadImages()
    checkload()
    animate()
</SCRIPT>
</BODY>
</HTML>
```

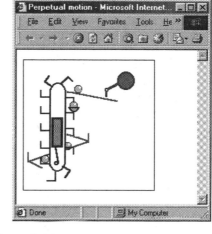

Figure 7.3 My perpetual
motion machine and its
image files. You can see it
in action on the JavaScript
Sampler page of my site:
http://homepages.tcp.co.uk/~macbride

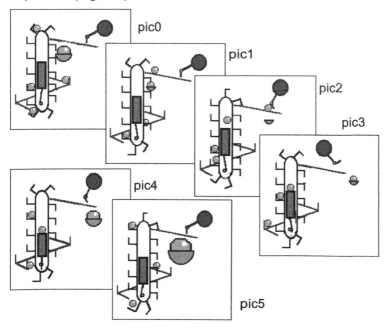

Controlled animation

The next example builds on the last by adding a set of control buttons. These allow the user to run the 'machine' at full speed or to step through the sequence, either forward or in reverse. Though there are five new control buttons, there are only two new functions. *nextpic()* changes the image to the next one forward or back, depending on the value of *move* (1 or –1).

```
function nextpic()
{
    current += move
    if (current <0)
        current  = 5
    if (current> 5)
        current  = 0
    pagePic.src =pictures[current].src
}
```

The Back and Next buttons set the move direction and call *nextpic()*.

```
<INPUT TYPE = button VALUE = " Back "
    onClick = "move = -1; nextpic()">
```

There is a new version of *animate()*. This is only concerned with keeping things moving, as the change of image is now handled by *nextpic()*. Notice the use of the *going* variable. If this is true, there is already a timeout set to run *animate()*, so this must be cleared before running the function again and setting another timeout. Miss it out and watch what happens if you click the **Run** or **Reverse** button more than once.

```
function animate()
{
    if (going)
        clearTimeout(timer)
    nextpic()
    timer = setTimeout("animate()",100)
}
```

To start it off, we just need to set *going* to true, assign a value to *move*, and call *animate()* for the first time.

```
<INPUT TYPE = button VALUE = " Run "
    onClick = "going = true; move = 1; animate()">
```

Here's the full code. It's a bit on the long side, but the last example will serve as a base and you can cut and paste when setting up the buttons.

```
<HTML>
<HEAD>
  <TITLE>Perpetual motion </TITLE>
  <SCRIPT>
  function loadImages()
  {
      pic0 = new Image()
      pic0.src = "pic0.gif"
      pic1 = new Image()
      pic1.src = "pic1.gif"
      pic2 = new Image()
      pic2.src = "pic2.gif"
      pic3 = new Image()
      pic3.src = "pic3.gif"
      pic4 = new Image()
      pic4.src = "pic4.gif"
      pic5 = new Image()
      pic5.src = "pic5.gif"
      pictures = new Array(pic0,pic1,pic2,pic3, pic4, pic5)
  }
  function nextpic()
  {
     current += move
     if (current <0)
        current  = 5
     if (current> 5)
        current  = 0
     pagePic.src =pictures[current].src
  }
   function animate()
  {
     if (going)
        clearTimeout(timer)
           nextpic()
     timer = setTimeout("animate()",100)
  }
```

```
      function checkload()
      {
          if (pic5.complete == false)
              setTimeout("checkload()", 100)
      }
</SCRIPT>
</HEAD>
<BODY>
<H3>Perpetual motion?</H3>
<IMG SRC = "pic0.gif" NAME = pagePic>
<SCRIPT>
    current = 0
    timer = null
    going = false
    move = 1
    loadImages()
checkload()
</SCRIPT>
<FORM>
<INPUT TYPE = button VALUE = " Reverse "
    onClick = "going = true; move = -1; animate()">
```

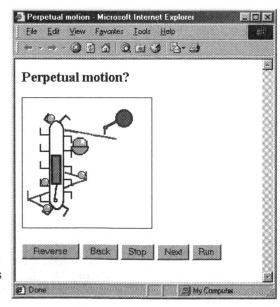

Figure 7.4 The machine with its added buttons.

```
<INPUT TYPE = button VALUE = " Back "
   onClick = "move = -1; nextpic()">
<INPUT TYPE = button VALUE = " Stop "
   onClick = "clearTimeout(timer)">
<INPUT TYPE = button VALUE = " Next "
   onClick = "move = 1; nextpic()">
<INPUT TYPE = button VALUE = " Run "
   onClick = "going = true; move = 1; animate()">
</BODY>
</HTML>
```

Clickable images

Images do not naturally react to the mouse, but they can be
made to do so with very little effort. If you enclose an image
with <A> tags, it takes on the properties of a link, which is
clickable.

A little care is needed. If the <A> tag is an HREF link and you
use the **onClick** event, like this…

```
<A HREF = www.wherever.com onClick = "dostuff()" >
<IMG SRC = "image1.gif"> </A>
```

… you may have a problem. After this code has executed the
dostuff() function it will link to the *wherever* site.

If you simply want to use the image to trigger some activity
within the page, there are two ways round this. One is to use
the **onMouseOver** event:

```
<A HREF = www.wherever.com onMouseOver = "dostuff()" >
<IMG SRC = "image1.gif"> </A>
```

This allows *dostuff()* to be activated without linking to the site,
but the image will still link when clicked.

The second – and better – approach is to use the <A> tag in its
simplest form, as an anchor. This responds to the mouse just as
a proper link does.

```
<A onClick = "dostuff()" > <IMG SRC = "image1.gif"> </A>
```

In the next example, the anchored image picks up three events.
onClick produces an alert showing the time; **onMouseOver**
and **onMouseOut** set messages in the Status line.

```
<HTML>
<HEAD>
<TITLE>Clickable image </TITLE>
<SCRIPT>
  function showtime()
  {
      d = new Date()
      h = d.getHours()
      m = d.getMinutes()
      s = d.getSeconds()
      alert("The time is now: " + h + ((m<10) ? ":0" : ":") +
  m + ((s<10) ? ":0" : ":") + s)
  }
  function setStatus(n)
  {
     if (n==1)
        self.status = "Click to see the time"
     else
        self.status = "Clickable image test page"
  }
</SCRIPT>
</HEAD>

<BODY>
<A onClick = "showtime()" onMouseOver = "setStatus(1)"
onMouseOut = "setStatus(2)"><IMG SRC = "clock.gif"></A>
</BODY>
</HTML>
```

JavaScript image maps

If you have image maps on your pages, remember that the
<AREA>s are clickable, and that you can attach code to
their tags.

Exercises

1 Create a form with two text inputs and a button. Display a random number in one input and ask the user to copy it into the other. When the button is clicked, the code should check that the number has been copied correctly and show the time taken.

2 Create a set of three or more images, of the same size but varying in colour or shape. Place them in a line across or down the screen and store them in an array. Rotate the image files through the <IMG> tags to give the impression of movement.

Summary

◆ With timeouts you can measure and control when code is executed. If timeouts are repeated regularly, you can create animation effects.

◆ Text can be animated by rearranging the characters within a string.

◆ Images can be animated by storing the files in arrays, then cycling the elements through <IMG> tags.

◆ You should clear a repeated timeout before restarting it. If you do not, a second cycle of repeats will be started, creating faster animation.

◆ Images are not naturally 'clickable', but can be made to respond to the mouse by enclosing them in a link or an anchor tag.

08 windows and frames

In this chapter you will learn

- how to control windows
- about the javascript URL
- about working in frames

Window control

JavaScript gives you more control over windows than you get with HTML. You can open a new window – specifying its size if you like – and load in an existing page file, or write new HTML code for the page from within JavaScript. When you have more than one window open, you can switch the focus from one to another, and run code in one window which reads the data from and writes into any other window.

Code with care

The window control methods are not tolerant of errors! A space in the wrong place, or missing quotes can produce unpredictable results. If a line of code doesn't do what you expect, go over it character by character and compare it with the syntax for the method.

---

window.open()

The **open**() method lets you specify the size of the window and which frame components (scrollbars, title bar, menu bar, etc.) to include. The basic syntax is:

varname = window.open("URL","*winName*", "*components*")

Virtually every bit of this method is optional!

◆ *varname* is needed if you want to run any methods or access any properties of the window.

◆ *URL* is used to load in an existing page, if required.

◆ *winName* is only needed if the window will be used as a TARGET from code in another window.

◆ The *components* are **toolbar**, **location**, **directories**, **status**, **menubar**, **scrollbars**, **resizable** – all of which are made to appear by setting them to *yes*. Any not listed are turned off by default. **width** and **height** can also be set, and are measured in pixels. All of the settings are done in one string, separated by commas.

You must put quotes around the *URL*, *winName* and one pair around the whole *components* string. If you are not loading a page, type empty double quotes (""). If you do not want to give the window a name, but do want to specify components, you must likewise type empty quotes where the name would have gone.

Some examples of its use:

```
window.open("http://www.yahoo.com")
```

Simply opens a standard browser window and loads in the page.

```
win2 = window.open("", "NewWin", "width=300,
    height=400")
```

Opens an empty window, giving it a target name of *NewWin*, and a variable name of *win2*. The window will have no toolbar, status bar or other components, and will be 300 by 400 pixels.

```
win2 = window.open("mini.htm", "", "toolbar=yes,
    width=300, height=500")
```

Opens a window, with a toolbar only, 300 by 500 pixels, and displays the *mini.htm* page.

Filling the window

When opened, the window can display an existing page file, or you can use the write() method to define the contents at the time, varying them in response to some previous feedback from the visitor. It is possible – though hard work – to construct large and complex pages, entirely through write().

In this first example, a window is opened, not to display a page, but as a 'pop-up' which tells the visitor more about a link on the page. As you can see in the screenshot, pointing at a link opens the window – and pointing at **Close** in the pop-up window, closes it.

The opening code is all in the function *popup()*, which is called by the **onMouseOver** event of the links. This is the basic shape:

```
<A HREF = "http://www...page ref..."
onMouseOver = "popup('text to display')">...Link text...</A>
```

When the mouse passes over the link, the event handler calls *popup()*, passing it a string of text.

popup() opens a small window then uses write() to create the display. There are two lines. The first writes the text, embedded in <H4> tags.

```
win2.document.write ("<H4>" + words + "</H4>")
```

The second creates an anchor with the **onMouseOver** code.

```
win2.document.write ("<A onMouseOver = 'self.close()'>
Close</A>")
```

Notice that **close**() shuts a window – **self.close**() shuts the window that holds the expression.

```
<HTML>
<HEAD>
<TITLE>Popups!</TITLE>
<SCRIPT>
function popup(words)
{
    win2 = window.open("", "", "width=250,height=100")
    win2.document.write ("<H4>" + words + "</H4>")
    win2.document.write ("<A onMouseOver =
'self.close()'> Close</A>")
}
</SCRIPT>
</HEAD>
<BODY>
<H3>Useful Links</H3>
<A HREF = "http://homepages.tcp.co.uk/~macbride"
    onMouseOver = "popup('Come up and see me
sometime')">Mac's place</A>
<P>
<A HREF = "http://www.teachyourself.co.uk"
    onMouseOver = "popup('Be where you want to be with
Teach Yourself')">Teach Yourself</A>
<P>
<A HREF = "http://www.amazon.com"
    onMouseOver = "popup('The leading on-line book
store')">Amazon</A>
</BODY>
</HTML>
```

The javascript URL

Up to this point, all our JavaScript code has been run from event handlers or directly from a <SCRIPT>. There is another way. I have been ignoring it because it tends to produce untidy – and therefore hard to read – code. This approach revolves around the word 'javascript:' used in a link.

```
<A HREF = "javascript:command">
```

The **javascript:...** fits into the place where you would normally see an **http://...** expression. The *command* doesn't have to be one that opens windows and loads up pages, but as visitors expect links to do that, it may be as well to use it mainly – or only – for that purpose.

In the example, the **javascript:** calls up the function *openWin()*, passing to it the URL of a page.

```
<A HREF = "javascript:openWin('www.amazon.com')">
```

The URL is picked up by the parameter *winfile* and passed to the **window.open** method – the only line in this function.

```
window.open (winfile, "", "scrollbars=no, width=280,
height=370")
```

It would have been possible to open directly from the **javascript:** starter, but would have led to this rather lengthy expression:

```
<A HREF = "javascript:window.open ('www.amazon.com',
'', scrollbars=no, width=280,height=370')">
```

As the link also needs its display text and/or an image, plus the closing </A>, it would give you some very nasty code!

```
<HTML>
<HEAD>
<SCRIPT>
function openWin(winfile)
{
    window.open (winfile, "", "scrollbars=no, width=280,
height=370")
}
</SCRIPT>
</HEAD>
```

```
<BODY>
<H3>Useful Links</H3>
<A HREF = "javascript:openWin('homepages.tcp.co.uk/
~macbride')"> Mac's place</A>
<P><A HREF =
"javascript:openWin('www.teachyourself.co.uk')"> Teach
Yourself</A>
<P><A HREF = "javascript:openWin('www.amazon.com')">
Amazon</A>
</BODY>
</HTML>
```

Working in frames

For the most part, working in framed pages is exactly the same as in unframed ones, but there are a few nice little touches you can add to a framed system with JavaScript. Here are a couple.

Following the focus

The **onFocus** and **onBlur** events occur when a visitor enters and leaves a page. With simple pages, these are of little use. With a framed system, where your visitor can move between pages in the different frames, it is worth reacting to these events.

The next example uses a two-frame layout, with a navigation bar down the left, and the main display area to the right. Code in the navigation bar toggles the colours of the two areas so that the one in focus is white and the other is blue.

```
onBlur= "document.bgColor= 'blue';
    parent.display.document.bgColor ='white' "
onFocus= "document.bgColor= 'white';
    parent.display.document.bgColor = 'blue' "
```

parent refers to the enclosing **<FRAMESET>** document, where *display* is defined as the second frame.

Because there are only two frames here, it is sufficient to have the colour-setting code in just one frame – if this one isn't in focus, the other one must be. With three or more frames, the simplest approach is to write code into each document that changes its own colour only.

Remote control

The *scroll()* method will move a document in a window or frame, just as if you were using the standard Windows scrollbars. There is little advantage in implementing this on a simple page – it is easier to use the scrollbars. With a framed system there is an advantage – if you put your scroll controls in the navigation frame, along with the links, then your visitor can control the whole display from one place.

The method is used in the form:

document.scroll(*newX, newY*)

With the *newX* and *newY* values measured in pixels, counting from the top left of the page, e.g.

document.scroll(0,500)

This would scroll the page up by roughly one screenful on an 800 × 640 display. The following example uses a variable, *frametop* and adjusts this by 200 in the *scrollup()* and *scrolldown()* functions.

To implement this example, type in and save the two documents, but replacing the links to existing pages of your own. At least one of these should be long enough to test out the scrolling routines!

test.htm
```
<HTML>
<FRAMESET COLS = 30%,*>
<FRAME SRC = navigate.htm NAME = navbar>
<FRAME SRC = contents.htm NAME = display>
</FRAMESET>
</HTML>
```

navigate.htm
```
<HTML>
<HEAD>
<SCRIPT>
frametop = 0
function scrollup() {
    frametop = (frametop >= 200) ? frametop - 200 : 0
    parent.display.scroll(0,frametop)
}
```

```
function scrolldown() {
   frametop = frametop + 200
   parent.display.scroll(0,frametop)
}
</SCRIPT>
</HEAD>

<BODY BGCOLOR= 'white' onBlur= "document.bgColor=
'blue'; parent.display.document.bgColor ='white' "
onFocus= "document.bgColor= 'white';
parent.display.document.bgColor = 'blue' ">

<H2>Navigation bar</H2>
<A HREF = feedbck1.htm TARGET = display>Feedback
form</A>
<P>
<A HREF = prompts.htm TARGET = display>Prompts</A>
<P>
<A HREF = motion.htm TARGET = display>Simple anima-
tion</A>
<FORM>
<INPUT TYPE = button VALUE = " Up " onClick =
"scrollup()">
<INPUT TYPE = button VALUE = "Down" onClick =
"scrolldown()">
</FORM>
</BODY>
</HTML>
```

Exercise

1 Start from the feedback form example (page 119) and add
  a function, activated by a button, that will open a new
  window and display the input data in it.

  As well as giving practice in using windows, this also takes
  you further into handling data. There are two main
  problems:

  (i) The selections from the list and radio buttons will
      need to be converted into text – the simplest solution

is to store the option text in arrays and pick it out of there.

(ii) It is difficult to access the data in one document once you have opened a new document window. The best approach here is to copy the elements' values into variables before opening the new window.

Summary

♦ The **open()** method allows you to open a new window, specifying its size and features.

♦ When a window is no longer needed it can be shut down with the **close()** method.

♦ The **javascript** command can be written into an <A HREF …> tag in place of a URL and used to activate code.

♦ In a framed system, you can use the **onBlur** and **onFocus** events to respond to a visitor's movements in the frames.

09
reference section

Standard colour names

JavaScript recognizes over 140 names for colours. Some of these
are duplicate names for the same colours; others are so similar
that you can scarcely tell them apart. Removing those leaves us
with this reduced list.

aquamarine	gold	pink
beige	goldenrod	plum
black	gray	powderblue
blue	green	purple
blueviolet	greenyellow	red
brown	hotpink	rosybrown
cadetblue	indianred	royalblue
chartreuse	indigo	saddlebrown
chocolate	khaki	salmon
coral	lavender	sandybrown
cornflowerblue	lightblue	seagreen
crimson	lightgray	sienna
cyan	lightgreen	silver
darkgoldenrod	lime	skyblue
darkgray	limegreen	slateblue
darkkhaki	magenta	springgreen
darkolivegreen	maroon	steelblue
darkorchid	mediumblue	tan
darkseagreen	mediumpurple	teal
darkslateblue	midnightblue	tomato
darkslategray	navy	turquoise
darkturquoise	olive	violet
darkviolet	olivedrab	wheat
deeppink	orange	white
deepskyblue	orangered	yellow
dodgerblue	orchid	yellowgreen
forestgreen	peru	

Reserved words

These are words reserved by JavaScript for its own (current or possible future) use. You cannot use them for variable names, function names or labels.

abstract	int
boolean	interface
break	long
byte	native
case	new
catch	null
char	package
class	private
const	protected
continue	public
default	return
delete	short
do	static
double	super
else	switch
extends	synchronized
false	this
final	throw
finally	throws
float	transient
for	true
function	try
goto	typeof
if	var
implements	void
import	while
in	with
instanceof	

Special characters

Character	Meaning
\b	backspace
\f	form feed – for printing
\n	new line
\r	carriage return
\t	tab
\'	single quote
\"	double quote
\\	backslash character (\).
\x*XX*	character code given as two hexadecimal digits *XX* between 00 and FF, e.g. For example, the trademark symbol ™ has a character code 153, which is \x99 in hexadecimal.

Event handlers

Object	Event handlers	Object	Event handlers
Area	onMouseOut onMouseOver	Radio	onBlur onClick onFocus
Button	onBlur onClick onFocus	Reset	onBlur onClick onFocus
Checkbox	onBlur onClick onFocus	Select	onBlur onChange onFocus
FileUpload	onBlur onChange onFocus	Submit	onBlur onClick onFocus
Form	onReset onSubmit	Text	onBlur onChange onFocus onSelect
Frame	onBlur onFocus		
Image	onAbort onError onLoad	Textarea	onBlur onChange onFocus onSelect
Link/area	onClick onMouseOut onMouseOver	Window	onBlur onError onFocus onLoad onUnload
Password	onBlur onFocus		

The Math methods

abs(*num*) strips off any minus sign, so abs(-4) = abs(4) = 4

acos(*num*) gives the arc cosine (i.e. the angle for which *num* is the cosine), measured in radians.

asin(*num*) gives the arc sine (i.e. the angle for which *num* is the sine) measured in radians.

atan(*num*) gives the arc tangent (i.e. the angle for which *num* is the tangent) measured in radians.

atan2(*x,y*) gives the angle, in radians between the X axis and a line drawn from 0,0 to *x,y*.

ceil(*num*) rounds a decimal value up to the next integer, e.g. ccil(4.6) = 5.

cos(*angle*) the cosine of *angle*, given in radians

eval( ) returns a number from a string or calculation.

exp(*log*) converts a logarithm back into a number.

floor(*num*) rounds a decimal value down to the next integer, e.g. floor(4.6) = 4.

log(*num*) gives the logarithm of a number

max(*num1,num2*) compares two values and returns the highest.

min(*num1,num2*) compares two values and returns the lowest.

pow(*n,p*) raises *n* to the power of *p* ; e.g. pow(2,3) = 2^3 = 8

random() generates a random number in the range 0.0 to 1.0.

round(*num*) converts a number with a decimal fraction up or down to the nearest integer.

sin(*angle*) the sine of *angle*, given in radians

sqrt(*num*) gives the square root of a number

toString(*num*) converts a number to a string

valueOf(*object*) returns the numeric value, if any, of an object

tan(*angle*) the tangent of *angle*, given in radians

The Date methods

Date and time are measured in milliseconds – there are 86,400,000 in a day – counting +/– 100 million days from 1st January 1970, UTC (universal) or GMT (Greenwich Mean Time). Date values can be given in milliseconds, or as a string, and JavaScript recognizes all the standard formats.

getDate() gives the day of the month from the specified date.

getDay() gives the number of the day of the week, 0 = Sunday.

getFullYear() gives the year as a 4-digit number.

getHours() gives the hour.

getMilliseconds() gives the millisecond component of the date.

getMinutes() gives the minutes component of the date.

getMonth() gives the number of the month, 0 = January.

getSeconds() gives the seconds component of the date.

getTimezoneOffset() gives the difference between local time and UTC.

getYear() gives the year as a 2-digit number.

All **get...**() methods are used in the form:

    component = date.get*Component*()

All **get...**() methods have UTC equivalents, e.g. **getUTCDay**() gives the day number by UTC time, rather than local time.

All **get...**() methods have **set...**() equivalents, e.g. **setDay**() which set the component of the date variable.

parse() converts a date string into milliseconds since 1/1/1970.

toGMTString() converts a local date/time to a GMT date/time.

toLocaleString() converts a GMT date to a local date.

toString() converts a date value to a text string.

UTC() the UTC equivalent of **parse**().

The String methods

anchor() equivalent to setting an anchor in HTML, e.g.

```
myText = "Top of page"
document.write(myText.anchor("pagetop"))
```

is the same as:

```
<A NAME = "pagetop">Top of page</A>
```

big() equivalent to <BIG>

blink() equivalent to <BLINK>, which only works in Netscape.

bold() equivalent to <B>

charAt(*place*) returns character at *place*, counting from 0 at the start of the string.

charCodeAt(*place*) returns the Unicode number of the character at *place*.

s1.**concat(*s2,s3,...*)** joins the strings *s2*, *s3*, etc. to *s1*.

fixed() equivalent to <TTY> – sets a monospaced font.

fontcolor() equivalent to <FONT COLOR ...>

fontsize() equivalent to <FONT SIZE ...>

fromCharCode(*code, code,...*) forms a text string from the series of character codes.

indexOf(*searchtext*) looks for *searchtext* and returns the place number of the first match.

italics() equivalent to <I>

lastIndexOf(*searchtext*) looks for *searchtext* and returns the place number of the last match.

link() equivalent to creating a link in HTML, e.g.

```
showText = "My place"
url = "www.myplace.com"
document.write("Click to visit me at " + showText.link(url))
```

has the same effect as:

```
Click to visit me at <A HREF = "www.myplace.com">My place</A>
```

match(*regex*) searches through the string for text matching the *regex* regular expression (page 162). The method has several parameters.

replace(*regex, newString*) searches for text matching *regex* and replaces it with *newString*.

search(*regex*) equivalent to **indexOf**() but searching for a regular expression instead of plain text.

slice(*begin,end*) returns the substring, where *begin* and *end* are counted from 0.

small() equivalent to <SMALL>

split(*separator, limit*) splits a string into substrings, dividing at the *separator* character. If set, *limit* sets a limit to how many substrings are to be made.

strike() equivalent to <STRIKE>

sub() equivalent to <SUB>

substr(*begin, length*) returns a substring of *length* characters, starting at *begin*.

substring(*begin, end*) the same as *slice()*.

sup() equivalent to <SUP>

toLowerCase() converts a string to lower case characters.

toUpperCase() converts a string to capital letters.

RegExp

A RegExp object holds a *regular expression*. It can be used for finding and replacing text in strings. An object can be created by:

    RegExpVar = /pattern/flags

Or

    RegExpVar = new RegExp("pattern","flags")

Notice that /slashes/ are used around the pattern in a simple assignment, but "quotes" are used when an object is created with **new**.

The pattern is made up of literals and special characters – there are many of these, of which a few are covered below.

The *flags* are optional and can be set to control the matching. There are three:

  g   global match
  i   ignore case
  m   match over multiple lines.

For example, these both set up a variable called regtext which can be used to look for "abc" in any combination of upper and lower case letters.

    Regtext = /ab+c/i
    regtext = new RegExp("ab+c", "i")

Some characters have special meanings in regular expressions. There are lots of these. Here are some of the more useful ones.

\   Indicates that the next character is special, e.g. /\b/ or "\b" means match a word boundary.

.   (dot) matches any single character, e.g. /g.n/ matches "gin" and "gun".

*   Matches the *preceding* character 0 or more times, e.g. /Smithe*/ matches "Smith" and "Smithee", and /b.*/ matches anything beginning with "b".

[abcd] or [a-d] Matches any one of the enclosed characters. You can give the characters individually or specify a range by using a hyphen, e.g. [m-o] match the "m" in "game" and either of the "n"s in "tennis".

^   Look for a match at the beginning of the line of text, e.g. /^M/ matches the first "M" in "My name is Michael" but does not match the "M" in "my name is Michael".

$ Matches at the end of the line, e.g. /c$/ matches the "c" in "comic", but docs not match it in "coding".

(regex) Matches "regex" and stores the matching strings in the predefined array $[], as $1, $2, etc.

\d   Matches a digit, e.g. /\d/ matches "2" in "This pencil may be a 2B - or not."

The RegExp methods

exec() executes the search and if successful, returns a result array and updates the regexp object. If the match fails, exec() returns null. It is similar to **String.match**().

     regexp.exec([*str*])

test() simply searches for a match and returns true or false. This is virtually the same as **String.search**().

     regexp.test([*str*])

10 answers to exercises

Chapter 2

1 This is the basic shape, but with your own messages.

```
<HTML>
<HEAD>
<SCRIPT>
function text1(){
    document.form1.display.value = "This is message 1"
}
function text2(){
    document.form1.display.value = "This is message 2"
}
function text3(){
    document.form1.display.value = "This is message 3"
}
</SCRIPT>
</HEAD>
<BODY>
<FORM NAME = form1>
<INPUT TYPE = text NAME = display VALUE = ""><BR>
<INPUT TYPE = button VALUE = "Text 1" onClick = "text1()">
<INPUT TYPE = button VALUE = "Text 2" onClick = "text2()">
<INPUT TYPE = button VALUE = "Text 3" onClick ="text3()">
</FORM>
</HTML>
```

2 The new functions should look like this.

```
function greenonblue()
{
    document.bgColor = "navy"
    document.fgColor = "lime"
}
function whiteonwhite()
{
    document.bgColor = "White"
    document.fgColor = "White"
}
```

3 The lines should look like this, and be written in
  <SCRIPT> tags in the BODY area. I have used <BR> to
  make the line break, but <P> could be used instead.

```
document.write("<H1>This is a big heading</H1>")
document.write("<H2>This is a smaller heading</H2>")
document.write("Here is a line of text<BR>")
document.write("And here is the next line")
```

Chapter 3

1 You should have something like this:

```
<SCRIPT>
    a = 4
    b = 3
    c = a + b
    document.write("The answer is " + c)
</SCRIPT>
```

2 The equation translates to this – the brackets ensure that the calculations are performed in the right order:

```
ans = ((10 + 6) / 4) * ((10 - 4) / 3)
```

3 The simplest solution is to repeat the loop that is used to write the names at the start of the output section:

```
for (dwarf = 0 ; dwarf < 7; dwarf++)
        document.write(nickname[dwarf] + "<BR>")
```

Chapter 4

1 The trick here is to use the outer loop to set the end value for the inner loop:

```
<SCRIPT>
    for (rows = 1; rows<11; rows++)
    {
        for(cols = 1; cols <= rows; cols++)
                document.write(" * ")
        document.write("<BR>")
    }
</SCRIPT>
```

2 A **while** loop is the best structure to use for this.

```
<SCRIPT>
    count = 10
    while(count>=0)
```

```
{
        document.write(count + "<BR>")
        count--
}
document.write("We have lift-off")
</SCRIPT>
```

3 A **do...while** loop handles this neatly.

```
<SCRIPT>
    x = Math.round(Math.random()*100)
    max = 100
    min = 0
    count = 0
    do
    {
        guess = prompt("What is my number?","")
        count++
        if (guess > x)
        {
                alert(" Too high")
                max = guess
        }
        if (guess < x)
        {
                alert(" Too low")
                min = guess
        }
    }
    while (guess != x)
    document.write("<BR> Found it in " + count + " goes.")
</SCRIPT>
```

4 Here is one solution. This uses an **if...else if ... else** structure.

```
<SCRIPT>
    category = "Standard"
    rate = 50
    age = prompt("Please enter age","")
    if (age <= 16)
    {
        category = "Junior"
```

```
            rate = 10
    }
    else if (age >= 65)
    {
            category = "Senior"
            rate = 15
    }
    else
    {
            working = prompt("Are you in work (Y/N)","")
            if (working == "N")
            {
                    category = "Concession"
                    rate = 20
            }
    }
    document.write("Your membership category is " +
category + " and the rate is " + rate)
</SCRIPT>
```

Chapter 5

1 The cube() function is easily extended – the only real
   changes are to bring in the power as a parameter, and to
   use that as the end value for the multiplying loop.

```
function myPower(num,pow)
{
    ans = 1
    for (count = 1; count <= pow; count++)
            ans = ans * num;
    return ans
}
```

2 There are several ways to do this. This one uses ceil().

```
function dice()
{
    return Math.ceil(Math.random() * 6)
}
```

3 The basis of this is to work through the length of the
   string character by character, copying them in to a new

string in reverse order. This can then be compared to the original string.

```
function palindrome(inString)
{
    len = inString.length
    backwards = new String()
    for (loop = 0; loop < len; loop++)
    {
        backwards = inString.charAt(loop) + backwards
    }
    if(inString == backwards)
        return true
    else return false
}
```

Chapter 6

1   If the function is only needed to check this specific input, the upper and lower limits can be written directly into it.

```
function validnum()
{
    price = document.form1.price.value
    if ((price < 1) || (price > 25))
        return false
    else return true
}
```

If you want to be able to use the same function to check difference numeric inputs, the upper and lower limits, and the value to be checked must be given as parameters.

```
function validnum(num, low,high)
{
    if ((num.value < low) || (num.value > high))
        return false
    else return true
}
```

Here's the calling code for this function:

... onBlur = "if(validnum(this,1,25)==false) ...

2   The possibilities here are endless! The test is does it work?

3 Your code should be along these lines.

```
<HTML>
<HEAD>
<SCRIPT>
link = new Array(4)
    link[0] = "www.netscape.com"
    link[1] = "devedge.netscape.com/central/javascript"
    link[2] = "developer.netscape.com"
    link[3] = "www.w3.org"
function setURL()
{
    where =document.form1.choice.selectedIndex
    window.location = link[where]
}
</SCRIPT>
</HEAD>
<BODY>
<H3>Useful JavaScript links</H3>
<FORM NAME = form1>
<SELECT NAME = choice>
<OPTION = netscape>Netscape home site
<OPTION = central>JavaScript Central
<OPTION = developer>Netscape Developer site
<OPTION = w3>W3 Consortium
</SELECT>
<P> <INPUT TYPE = button VALUE = "Go for it" onClick =
"setURL()">
</FORM>
</BODY>
</HTML>
```

Chapter 7

1 Here is one solution. The *marktime()* function is called
when the page is loaded and repeats every second,
incrementing *counter*. check() compares the *input* with the
display number and reports the time elapsed.

```
<HTML>
<HEAD>
<SCRIPT>
```

```
function marktime() {
    counter++
    timer = setTimeout("marktime()",1000)
}
function check() {
    clearTimeout(timer)
    if (form1.input.value == form1.display.value)
        alert("Correct in " + counter + " seconds")
    else alert("Mistyped in " + counter + " seconds")
}
</SCRIPT>
</HEAD>
<BODY>
<FORM NAME = form1>
Type this: <INPUT TYPE = text NAME = display>
<P>In this box: <INPUT TYPE = text NAME = input>
<P><INPUT TYPE = button VALUE = Done onClick =
"check()">
</FORM>
<SCRIPT>
    counter = 0
    form1.display.value = Math.round(Math.random() *
1000000)
    marktime()
</SCRIPT>
</BODY>
</HTML>
```

2   Here is one possible solution. The central part of this is
    the *animate()* function which rotates the images through
    the <IMG> tags. Notice the line:

```
index = (index < 2) ? ++index : 0
```

This switches *index* between 0, 1 and 2 – if *index* is less
than 2, it is incremented, otherwise it is set to 0. The line
is repeated for every image, so that each accesses a different element of the array. **index**-- at the end ensures that
index has a different start value the next time round.

```
<HTML>
<HEAD>
<SCRIPT>
```

```
function loadImages()
{
    pic0 = new Image()
    pic0.src = "reddart.gif"
    pic1 = new Image()
    pic1.src = "bluedart.gif"
    pic2 = new Image()
    pic2.src = "grndart.gif"
}
function animate()
{
    if (going)
        clearTimeout(timer)
    index = (index < 2) ? ++index : 0
    document.images[index].src = pic0.src
    index = (index < 2) ? ++index : 0
    document.images[index].src = pic1.src
    index = (index < 2) ? ++index : 0
    document.images[index].src = pic2.src
    index--
    if (going)
        timer = setTimeout("animate()",200)
}
</SCRIPT>
</HEAD>
<BODY>
<SCRIPT>
    var timer = null
    var going = false
    loadImages()
    index = 0
</SCRIPT>
<IMG SRC="reddart.gif">
<IMG SRC="grndart.gif">
<IMG SRC="bluedart.gif">
<FORM>
<INPUT TYPE = "button" VALUE = "Roll em"
onClick = "going = true; animate()">
<INPUT TYPE = "button" VALUE = "Stop"
onClick = "going = false; animate()">
```

```
</FORM>
</BODY>
</HTML>
```

Chapter 8

1 Here is one solution. The *marktime()* function is called

```
regionName = new Array(5)
regionName[0] =" London"
regionName[1] = "South East"
regionName[2] = "South West"
regionName[3] = "Rest of England"
regionName[4] = "Wales"


coverType = new Array(3)
coverType[0] = "Third Party"
coverType[1] = "Third Party Fire and Theft"
coverType[2] = "Comprehensive"


function check()
{
   Cvalue = document.form1.InsVal.value
   Cregion =
regionName[document.form1.region.selectedIndex]
   for(loop = 0; loop < 3; loop++)
         if (document.form1.cover[loop].checked)
               Ccover =coverType[loop]
   Cquote = document.form1.quote.value

   win2 = window.open("", "", "width=400,height=250")
   win2.document.write ("<H4> Your details </H4>")
   win2.document.write ("<P> Cycle value: " + Cvalue )
   win2.document.write ("<P> Region: " + Cregion )
   win2.document.write ("<P> Type of cover: " + Ccover)
   win2.document.write ("<P> Quoted cost: " +
Cquote+"</P>" )
   win2.document.write ("<INPUT TYPE = button VALUE
= 'Close' onClick = 'self.close()'>")
}
```

taking it further

This book was never intended to be a complete course in JavaScript, but it has, I hope, given you a good grounding in the language and the confidence to go on further.

So where do you go from here? There are two main routes of development. The first comes from within you. Master what you have learnt and bring your creativity to bear. Play with the components of JavaScript and see what you can construct with them. What do you want to say, and how can you say it with what you know? The second route looks beyond. What other tools, techniques and languages are available to the JavaScript programmer? What are other people doing? What can you learn from more experienced page builders?

The Web offers lots of information, samples and services for JavaScript programmers. Here are just a few selected sites.

DevEdge

http://devedge.netscape.com/

The main Netscape-based site for Web developers, and as Netscape was behind JavaScript, it is also the main site for all JavaScript users. At some point, download the Core JavaScript Guide – run a search for it or type in this path:

.../library/manuals/2000/javascript/1.5/guide

You should also get the Core JavaScript Reference from:

.../library/manuals/2000/javascript/1.5/reference

The JavaScript Source

http://javascript.internet.com/

A good place to start to explore JavaScript, with lots of examples to cut and paste.

JavaScript.com

http://javascript.com/

Claims to be the definitive JavaScript resource, and is certainly well worth visiting. It has tutorials, reference guides, articles, tips and examples.

JavaScript Kit

http://javascriptkit.com/

A good source of examples (nearly 800!), with tutorial articles on aspects of programming. The site also has good links to other types of Web page programming, if you want to start exploring beyond JavaScript.

JavaScript City

http://javascriptcity.com/

Another good site with plenty of examples, tutorials and other resources.

Web Monkey

http://hotwired.lycos.com/webmonkey/

A great resource for developers in any programming language, but look for the JavaScript Library in particular.

index

teach yourself

the internet
mac bride

- Are you keen to explore the internet with confidence?
- Do you want to get the latest news and information?
- Do you need to do business or go shopping online?

The Internet is a clear, jargon-free introduction for anyone who wants to understand the internet and exploit its rich potential. This book will help you to explore the world wide web, communicate via email, find the information you need, shop or play games online and set up your own home page.

Mac Bride is the author of many top-selling programming and computer application books, and brings over 20 years of teaching experience to his writing.

teach yourself

html: publishing on the www
mac bride

- Are you an Internet user?
- Do you want to move from browsing to publishing?
- Do you want to explore the possibilities of HTML?

HTML: Publishing on the WWW takes the mystery out of the technical issues and jargon on web site building. It covers the whole of HTML, from the very basics through to style sheets, clearly explained and with worked examples throughout. With this book you can learn enough to create a colourful, illustrated web page in just a few hours, or put together a full-featured, interactive, interlinked web site in a few days.

Mac Bride is the author of many top-selling programming and computer application books, and brings over 20 years of teaching experience to his writing.

teach
yourself

C++
richard riley

- Are you new to programming?
- Do you need to improve your existing C++ skills?
- Do you want to become an expert programmer?

C++ is a concise guide to programming in C++, one of the most popular and versatile languages in use today. All the concepts and techniques you need to create powerful programs are clearly explained, with examples and revision exercises used throughout.

Richard Riley is a computer programmer who has written extensively in C++, Perl, Java, JavaScript and HTML.